MARCO POLO
TENERIFE
GOMERA AND HIERRO

with Local Tips

The author's special recommendations are highlighted in yellow throughout this guide

There are six symbols to help you find your way around this guide:

★

for Marco Polo recommendations - the best in each category

for all the sites with a great view

for places frequented by the locals

♀

where young people get together

(A1)

map references

for the perfect tour of Tenerife follow the yellow route

MARCO ⊕ POLO

Other travel guides and language guides in this series:

Algarve • Amsterdam • Brittany • California • Crete • Cyprus
Florida • Gran Canaria • New York • Paris • Prague
Mallorca • Rhodes • Rome • Turkish Coast
French • German • Spanish • Italian

*Marco Polo would be very interested to hear your
comments and suggestions. Please write to:*

*World Leisure Marketing Ltd
Marco Polo Guides
9 Downing Road, West Meadows
Derby DE21 6HA England*

*Cover photograph: 'The finger of God', Pico del Teide (Schuster/Kasch)
Photographs: Baumli (4, 12, 22, 28, 32, 50, 66, 72); Kallabis (62); Lade: BAV (41);
Lindner (16); Mauritius: Beck (48), Leblond (7, 76), Mehlig (8), Murillo (83),
Nägele (55), Schwanke (30), Vidler (inside front cover); Nowaczyk (14);
Schapowalow: Huber (85); Transglobe: Merten (69, 71), Mollenhauer (86),
Svensson (26); Touristik-Marketing GmbH(34)
Cartography: Mairs Geographischer Verlag, Hallwag*

*1st English edition 1997
© Mairs Geographischer Verlag, Ostfildern Germany
Authors: Dieter Nowaczyk and Hannelore Lindner
Translation: Paul Fletcher
English edition: Cathy Muscat, Emma Kay
Editorial director: Ferdinand Ranft
Design and layout: Thienhaus/Wippermann
Printed in Italy*

CONTENTS

Discover Tenerife

Where the sea and the mountains, tropical forest and arid desert combine to create an island of charm and contrast

The largest and perhaps the most beautiful of the Canary Islands, Tenerife has everything the traveller needs to fulfil holiday dreams. It is an island of spectacular contrasts, with majestic volcanoes, vast banana plantations, stretches of desert, pine forests and fertile valleys interspersed with traditional villages, busy towns and bustling tourist resorts. The flat coastal plains, light sandy beaches, the blue Atlantic and almost perpetual sun offer an irresistible year-round invitation. Whatever you are looking for in a holiday destination, you will find it here. The miles of coastline, plus some magnificent waves, make this spot ideal for watersports enthusiasts, while windsurfers and sailors head for the south of the island, where the wind is strong and steady. Sun-worshippers and beach-lovers will not be disappointed either. There is rarely a cloud in the sky and the island is scattered with

This ancient dragon tree in Icod de los Vinos has become a symbol for Tenerife

sandy beaches and isolated coves. For outdoor adventurers, there is a whole network of country paths, large areas of magnificent woodland to explore, and the mountains, which are cut through with wild and romantic gorges, are perfect for climbing. In the winter months, there's even snow to be found at altitudes of 2000 m and higher. Apart from all its natural beauty Tenerife has an active night-life. There are plenty of opportunities to wind down after a hard day's exploring or sunbathing and for the steadfast nocturnals, there is no shortage of clubs that stay open until the small hours.

Travellers flying into Tenerife for the first time will peer down from the tiny cabin window to catch a first glimpse of this volcanic island in the Atlantic – and may well be disappointed by what they see, or rather, don't see. Apart from a band of clouds hovering above the island, hardly any of its attractions are visible. Even after landing, you may look around and wonder whether you have accidentally arrived at the wrong place. After the four-hour

HISTORY AT A GLANCE

1100-800 BC
The Phoenicians were probably the first people to set foot on the Canary Islands

1341
Island rediscovered by Portuguese seafarers

1402
Jean de Béthencourt sets out to conquer the archipelago for the Castilian throne

1477
Catholic kings charge Alonso Fernández de Lugo with the task of conquering the still independent islands of Gran Canaria, Tenerife and La Palma

9 August 1492
While on his voyage of discovery, Christopher Columbus sails past the island and records the eruption of the Teide volcano

1494
The Spanish land on the beach at Añaza, now Santa Cruz. Peace negotiations with the Guanches fail

1495
The Spanish defeat the Guanches at La Victoria. Tenerife is the last of the Canary Islands to fall into Spanish hands

16th century
Tenerife is colonized and the Guanches are introduced to Christianity. Sugar cane is cultivated and processed

17th century
Vines for wine production are planted, after sugar cane turns out to be unprofitable

1704/05/06
Serious volcanic eruptions

1715
Wine production in crisis and many of the islanders emigrate to Latin America

1774
La Laguna becomes the island's first university town

1797
During an attack on his fleet at Santa Cruz, Admiral Nelson loses his right arm

1852
The Canary Islands are divided into two provinces: Santa Cruz de Tenerife and Las Palmas de Gran Canaria

from 1870
With the successful application of aniline dyes, Tenerife's cochineal farming industry collapses and thousands more islanders emigrate

1888
First banana plantation

18 July 1936
General Francisco Franco, the military commander of the Canary Islands, flees Santa Cruz to Morocco and the Spanish Civil War begins

from 1960
Tourism takes over as the most important sector in the local economy

1982
The two Canary Island provinces become autonomous regions

flight from northern Europe's chilly climes, you emerge from the Reina Sofía airport to be confronted with a desert-like landscape fringed with bare, volcanic peaks, where dusty cacti and parched shrubs bake in the sun. The vegetation has all the hallmarks of the Saharan desert, which is actually only 300 km away. But don't be dismayed – the golden beaches and crystal clear waters are closer than they seem.

The two main holiday centres on the island, Playa de las Américas and Los Cristianos, the ultimate destinations for the majority of visitors, are only a few kilometres from the airport, on the eastern side of the island's southern tip. Although not renowned for its scenic beauty, this region does have its own appeal, though this has more to do with the superb watersports facilities and nightlife on offer than its natural charms.

The road that heads due north from the airport hugs the coastline as it wends its way through a sandy, stony landscape. It then veers westward and suddenly, after just an hour's drive, the surroundings are miraculously transformed and you find yourself entering a different environment altogether. This side of the island conceals a whole new world bursting with colour, one of outstanding natural beauty. It soon becomes clear why the island is sometimes referred to as the 'Island of Eternal Spring'. The lush green of the banana plantations, verdant woodland and an ever-changing variety of multi-

Prickly pears have flourished on Tenerife for centuries

coloured vegetation extend for miles across the whole of northern Tenerife.

The central massif, the Cumbre Dorsal, clearly visible as it emerges from the clouds, divides the island into two distinct zones: the dry, barren south and the rich, fertile north. In the north the sunny climate, mineral-rich soil and constant gentle north-easterly trade winds provide ideal conditions for the abundance of flora, generating a fantastic plant growth rate. The moist air that blows in from the ocean collides with the mountainsides and cools as it rises. Consequently, along the northern slopes, at altitudes of between 700 and 1700 m, clouds form during the morning and then usually disperse during the course of the afternoon. However, these clouds rarely burst – nature receives their moisture in the form of mist and condensation. On the lee side of the mountains, the trade winds turn into dry, downhill winds. These help to reduce temperatures in the south, which would otherwise be two to four degrees higher. Nowhere else in the world do these unique climatic conditions exist. They bestow on the island well-balanced temperatures, which in the summer range from 18 to 24°C and in the winter average between 16 and 20°C, thus making Tenerife a good holiday destination at any time of year. Even when the mercury rises, the heat is never very oppressive, as the constant trade winds help to reduce its intensity. In the evening, the air remains mild and pleasantly cool. Winter temperatures rarely drop below 14°C. It was with good reason that the explorer Anderson, who was a member of Captain Cook's third expedition party, advised doctors to send their ailing patients to Tenerife to recuperate.

Tall poinsettias line the island paths and roads

Time for a siesta

The Canary Islanders are not slaves to the clock – they are masters of it. Rushing around non-stop is not the Canarian way. Standing at length in a queue at the post office or at the bank is part of everyday life and holidaymakers are advised to exercise the same degree of patience. In the rural parts of the island, an afternoon siesta is still very much a part of daily routine and this is the time when you will have to contend with the locals' relaxed attitude to life. Buses run late, churches and small museums close and bar-owners doze in front of their television screens. If you can adapt to this way of life, you will enjoy a more relaxing holiday than someone who is unable to make a change from the more frenetic pace of life back home.

For many holidaymakers, the diversity of the landscape is one of Tenerife's main attractions. The bizarre lunar landscape that emerges at an altitude of about 2000 m is captivating. Congealed trails, blocks of lava in weird shapes and shimmering colours dominate the scenery, serving as an object lesson in volcanology. Out of this strange and atmospheric setting rises Tenerife's highest mountain, the Pico del Teide (3718 m) – the highest peak on Spanish soil.

In the north-east of the island the landscape suddenly changes and the unexpected contrast is quite breathtaking. Here you'll discover the fissured rocks of the Anaga mountain range, a peninsula which rises up dramatically from the Atlantic. The Teno hills in the north-west are no less impressive. This severe, inaccessible world is blanketed with colourful plant life. Down in the valleys lie sleepy villages that the tourist who sticks to the beaten track would almost certainly miss, but for keen walkers and mountain climbers and those looking for

the authentic Tenerife, these represent the closest thing to paradise and make a good starting-point for exploring the varied countryside. Along the north of the island, the scenery unfolds and changes as if in a film. The stunning wilderness of the mountain region suddenly cuts to the bright green of a seemingly impenetrable woodland of laurel, eucalyptus, pines and firs.

The fertile soil in the north of the island yields a rich harvest in both summer and winter. Cereals, tomatoes, potatoes, maize, grapes and a wide range of fruit flourish on the hillsides. Many fruits grow to a size that would make any self-respecting market gardener turn green with envy.

What is so fascinating about Tenerife is that, on a surface area of only 2057 sq km, as many different types of landscape occur as would normally be found on a continental land mass. Tenerife also boasts a number of indigenous plants and flowers that don't grow anywhere else in the world. Red and violet bougainvillaea run wild like weeds, brightening up house walls and street scenes, while the poinsettia, known to many Europeans as a Christmas pot plant, grows into a bush three to four metres in height. Tourists who are impressed by the beauty of the *strelitzia* (bird-of-paradise flower) can buy them as presents ready-packed for the flight home. These floral marvels are not just confined to the rural areas, they thrive in every environment and relieve the monotony of the concrete landscapes that prevail in the main holiday resorts.

Observant travellers will enjoy exploring the artistic and architectural delights of the island's towns and villages. Traditional Canarian wooden balconies adorn many of Tenerife's original buildings. Other items of historic interest include art works and excavated artifacts that shed light on the island's history and its first inhabitants, the Guanches, about whom we still know very little. What we do know is that these were a proud and peace-loving people, characteristics that are still evident in today's *Canarios*, despite centuries of inbreeding since the arrival of the Spanish conquistadors. The islanders are helpful and friendly – on first meeting, they come across as open and extremely hospitable. On this island, very few people regard punctuality as a virtue, and you should not let yourself become exasperated by what seems to be a stubborn indifference to time. The *Canarios* will treat foreigners in different ways depending on which social strata they originate from, or whether they live in the towns or in the country. The more rural the setting, the more straightforward the *Canarios*

seem, particularly the older inhabitants who live life at a different pace as they sit outside their front doors, impassive but satisfied with their lot and seemingly unaware of the rapid changes that have taken place in their world. It is no longer possible to ignore the lines of hotels in the south of the island or in Puerto de la Cruz, the main resort in the north. The relentless construction that mushroomed in the early 1960s drew increasing numbers of tourists with pockets full of hard currencies to Puerto, and in just three decades its population has increased to about 27 000. The town has a cosmopolitan feel, characterized by a colourful blend of tourists and inhabitants from many different cultures including *Canarios*, mainland Spanish, Indian and Arab traders. But despite such radical changes, the old town retains some of its original charm in a maze of narrow streets and alleys and in its squares, where the locals enjoy siestas in the shade of tall laurels and palms. The contrast is stark between the old and the new. Traditional Canarian houses with ornate wooden balconies and the tranquil old fishing port, where anglers peacefully while away the hours, stand out against the brash hotels, crowds of tourists and streets jammed with traffic. But anyone who wishes to escape briefly from the hustle and bustle of thriving international tourism can easily find refuge in the nearby parks, flower gardens and other sanctuaries.

Tenerife can also offer a wealth of leisure and entertainment possibilities for visitors in search of a break from the everyday routine of work. Just why do three million outsiders, mainly northern Europeans, descend on this island each year? The enticing climate is certainly one reason, but it is just as likely to be because Tenerife offers more than the holiday brochures can describe, more than the tour operators and travel agencies can provide. For many, this island has become something of a winter residence. But this does not mean that Tenerife is suited only to senior citizens – quite the opposite. Young people find the island an ideal spot for countless activities. In addition to every imaginable watersport, such as sailing, diving, windsurfing, surfing and water-skiing, activities such as riding, golf and tennis are as popular as walking or fishing. And those in search of a lively night-life will certainly get their money's worth. In some resorts you will even find English-language theatre productions; many hotels also put on cabarets for English speaking guests. Throughout the year, locals from the neighbouring towns and villages stage a variety of festivals. Tenerife's original inhabitants revelled in song and dance and the descendants of the Guanches have added games and wrestling to these traditions. Characterized by lively rhythms and energetic dance movements, the *Canarios'* festivals provide excellent opportunities to discover the traditions and convivial nature of the islanders. The biggest, most colourful and most extravagant of the Canarian calendar's annual events is the Shrovetide carnival, Mardi Gras, an occasion of such festivity

that it could certainly rival the exuberance of the legendary carnival in Rio.

It will eventually become apparent that the north coast of Tenerife has one drawback: there are no beaches. When the island was formed as a result of volcanic activity, the north coast was left with a steep, rocky shoreline that is, in most places, quite difficult to reach. In Puerto de la Cruz, however, two large beach areas have recently been made accessible – Playa Jardín and Playa Martiánez; the latter also has an artificial seawater swimming-pool nearby. Other features along this stretch of coastline are the *barrancos*, canyon-style gorges that cleave the hillsides as they roll down to the sea. In the winter months, when the weather can turn very stormy, waves as high as houses thunder in, creating an impressive natural spectacle. Equally amazing (although in a completely different way) are the island's romantic sunsets, when the rocks are briefly bathed in glowing colour as the sun rapidly disappears beyond the Atlantic horizon.

Many visitors find that Tenerife makes an ideal base for island-hopping. You can catch a plane from the northern airport to travel to the neighbouring islands of La Palma and Hierro in the west, or else take a ferry across to Gomera, the nearest island to Tenerife. If you have a bit of time on your hands, try to explore the more barren, eastern islands of Gran Canaria, Lanzarote and Fuerteventura. Doing so is the best way to get a vivid impression of the amazing contrasts between the seven islands.

Guanches and dragon trees

The largest of the Canary Islands boasts a wealth of natural beauty, including Spain's highest mountain

African heat

Two to three times a year, nearly always in autumn and spring, a hot wind blows across to the Canary Islands from the Sahara Desert, bringing rust-red sand and dust with it. The locals call this sirocco wind *el tiempo de África*. The heat reduces humidity on the islands to almost zero and the temperature can rise to 45°C. The first signs of an approaching storm are wisps of reddish dust passing over the island's peaks. These particles get everywhere, into the tiniest cracks and crevices, but the gusts of wind are the greatest cause for concern as they can devastate whole plantations. In the tourist areas, the buildings weaken the power of the wind and the coastal areas do not suffer so badly from the low humidity levels. Salvation usually comes to man and nature after three to five days, in the form of heavy rain that chases away the strong winds.

The inner courtyard of a traditional Canarian house in La Orotava

Agriculture

Even in Tenerife, young people are choosing to leave their villages and are heading for the tourist centres and the main towns in search of employment, allowing acres of fertile land to fall into the hands of speculators. Nevertheless, agriculture still plays an important part in the island's economy and social structure. The agricultural history of Tenerife serves as a warning to many of today's farmers that one-crop farming often leads to disaster. In the past, international factors have contributed to crises in the cultivation of sugar cane, vines, prickly pears (for breeding the cochineal, an insect used to produce red dye) and bananas, so in more recent times, the island farmers have switched to mixed farming. Diversification is now the watchword and bananas, tomatoes, oranges, potatoes, avocado pears, wine, strawberries and flowers are today's mainstays of the agricultural industry. Banana cultivation is still predominant, but given the rising production costs and the strong competition from central America,

13

A typical Tenerife house with carved wooden balconies

trade in this fruit is suffering. The plantations are to be found mainly in the lower-lying regions along the north coast and in the south-west. Cultivating banana trees requires much careful work, as the soil needs to be tended and plenty of water is essential – it takes between 16 and 19 months before the tree bears fruit. About 95% of Tenerife's banana crop is imported by Spain. Elsewhere on the island, the steep hillsides have been terraced to assist crop cultivation, but soil erosion, a rocky sub-soil, water shortages and the baking sun make for back-breaking work. It is often impossible to bring tractors onto the slopes and a proper, extensive irrigation system is required. In the arid south, farmers still use the Canarian dry-field cultivation system. The soil is covered with porous, water-retaining basalt rock granules, which at night absorb water from the moist soil, thereby helping to prevent evaporation and erosion.

Alongside bananas, goats' cheese and a robust red wine are two other homegrown products that play a significant part in the island economy. Chickens, rabbits and pigs are bred to meet the local demand for meat, while flowers have become a lucrative export product. The bird-of-paradise flower (*strelitzia reginae*) is a popular souvenir for tourists.

Architecture

No destructive wars have taken place on Tenerife since the Spanish conquest and, because of the mild climate, weather damage to buildings is minimal. Consequently, many fine landowners' residences, churches, monasteries and houses from the 17th and 18th centuries have retained their original splendour. Soon after the island's conquest, the first churches appeared in Gothic style, but at the start of the 17th century, immigrants from Andalusia and Portugal began to build churches in the Mudéjar style. Visitors who explore the island thoroughly will discover that many churches were built during that period and the woodworkers' skills developed in parallel. Ornately carved balconies, often from precious teak which makes for a striking contrast with the white-washed walls, became a typical feature of house façades. The locals adopted the Spanish preference for building their houses around courtyards. Pretty gardens were laid out in these patios, which often included a fountain at the centre. The poorer people in the towns and in rural areas built single-storey, white-washed cottages, roofed with round red tiles, on a rectangular or L-shaped ground-plan, sometimes with decorative carvings on the doors and window frames. An irregular window arrangement usually indicates that the house was built in the 16th century; by the 17th century, a pattern of equal-sized windows with a door in the middle was becoming popular. At the beginning of the 19th century, Portuguese colonial-style baroque with its elaborate cast-iron balconies appeared, mainly in the towns. Town halls and municipal buildings were built in the neo-classical style during this period. The middle of the 20th century saw the arrival of tourism and that meant hurriedly erected, multistorey concrete blocks. The 'Lago de Martiánez' seawater swimming pools with islands and waterways built in Puerto de la Cruz, were designed by the Lanzarote artist and architect César Manrique, in a style which blends with the contours of the natural surroundings. Nowadays, buildings in neo-Canarian style exhibit the traditional wooden balconies and decorative stonework.

Carpets of flowers

When, in the middle of the 19th century, interest in the Corpus Christi procession in the Orotava valley waned, the aristocratic Señora del Castillo de Monteverde decided to revive the event by having a carpet of flowers laid in front of her house. Before long, a floral design with two doves suspended in the middle of an oval became the symbol for the procession. This new art form quickly won many followers and the tradition of lining the whole processional route with a carpet

of blossoms was soon established. Some 150 carts were required to bring in the bales of heather used in the creation of these intricate floral patterns. By singeing the heather to varying degrees, it is possible to achieve various shades of colour, ranging from green to black. In this way, the backdrop to the picture is prepared and then the picture itself is created by arranging the various blossoms on top. When King Alfons XIII visited La Orotava in March 1906, the town hall square was decorated with a carpet of blossoms for the first time. Felipe Machado y Benítez de Lugo soon became famous for his designs. He would start work a month before Corpus Christi and would integrate colourful pieces of lava into the picture. Dates, eucalyptus fruit, pieces of straw and vegetables were also included in the finished article. His grandson Tomás developed the idea by making a huge carpet measuring 870 square metres. Only one colour was used, but this colour changed according to the direction of the light. Today, the municipal academy of art still lays out the three-part carpet in front of La Orotava's town hall, and every year thousands of visitors flock here to admire the biblical scenes that have been so painstakingly and skilfully created. A similar display can be seen in La Laguna, where students lay out a floral carpet along the roads leading from La Concepción church to the cathedral.

The cultural scene

Tenerife may well be an isolated island, but that is no reason to assume that the islanders are cut off from world culture. Quite the reverse is true, as any visitor will see from the range of books available in the bookshops in the university town of La Laguna, Santa Cruz and Puerto de la Cruz. It is impossible to overlook the fact that practically all the important writers in the world whose works have been translated into Spanish are represented here. Anyone with a passing knowledge of Spanish can glance through the daily newspaper and find that a varied selection of courses, seminars and lectures are available and if you wish to learn something of the language and culture while you are here, you will not have much difficulty in finding a Spanish course for tourists. There is a popular saying which maintains that *Canarias es tierra de poetas* – 'The Canaries is a land of poets'. The beauty of the landscape, together with the inherent desire to discover wider horizons, has produced many a poet – Pedro Garcia Cabura, Marcel Rios Ruiz and Julio Tovar are among the most acclaimed. The inhabitants of Tenerife have wide and varied intellectual and artistic interests. The lively cultural scene on the island provides evidence of this. Many concerts, theatre and operatic performances are staged in the main towns. Unfortunately, visitors to the island who cannot understand Spanish will have to make do with the musical events.

Flora

The German naturalist Alexander von Humboldt declared that Tenerife was blessed with plants that bestowed greatness upon these lands near the equator. Between 1700 and 1800 different

Bronze statue of a Guanche king in Candelaria

species of plant grow on the Canary Islands, but only 400 of them are unique to Tenerife. Given the various climatic zones on the steep mountains, the vegetation can be divided into five categories according to the height of the land. Tropical and subtropical plants thrive below 600 m above sea level, and extensive banana plantations cover the lower slopes on the north side of the island. Eucalyptus trees, Canarian cedars, planes, mimosas, palisanders, rubber trees, blue-flowering jacaranda trees and various types of palms and laurels border the gardens, streets and squares. Hibiscus, bougainvillaea, tulip and orchid trees flower practically all the year round, while the poinsettia grow like weeds to a height of several metres. Roses of every colour, lilies, the white calla and the orange-flowering bird-of-paradise adorn many gardens. Cacti and agaves grow in the south, up to an altitude of 1000 m above sea level. Between 600 and 1500 m, fields of potatoes and cabbages are separated by chestnuts and eucalyptus groves. In the Anaga mountains, laurel woods with ferns, hollies and tree heath form a dense 'primeval forest'. Above 1500 m, wide expanses of pine forests provide shelter for broom, heathers, mushrooms and a number of plants unique to the Canary Islands. Above 2000 m, the endemic, exclusively Canarian varieties occur, 11 of which are only found in the Cañadas and on Mount Teide. One unusual species found on the Canary Islands is the dragon tree. It has hard, pointed leaves around a fan-shaped crown supported by a tall, rough trunk. It is a member of the Liliaceae family of plants and can grow to a height of 20 m. One especially grand example, which is now a permanent fixture on the Tenerife tourist route, is the dragon tree at Icod de los Vinos. It is said to be anywhere between 400 and 3000 years old, but dragon trees do not form annual rings, so its age can only be guessed from the number of branches – not an easy task, as new ones appear at irregular intervals. If you scratch at the bark, the resin that oozes out turns blood red. The Guanches used this 'dragon's blood' to embalm their dead.

Folklore

On Tenerife, the veneration of a patron saint or observation of a religious holiday is cause for celebration and that means, first and foremost, a solemn procession or a colourful parade. In the evening, jubilant music accompanied by dancing makes for a convivial gathering. Preparations start days in advance. The towns are decorated with brightly-coloured garlands and a stage is erected on the plaza. *Tinerfeños*, as the islanders call themselves, don their colourful costumes when they set off on a *romería*, a pilgrimage – most of these take place between May and August – or when they are participating in an event organized for tourists. Every region has its own type of costume. In the Orotava valley, for example, the women wear a brightly-coloured, striped dress that is gathered up at the sides, with a richly embroidered bodice and a headscarf topped by a small straw hat. The music betrays clear South American influences and is played on large castanets *(chácaras)*, guitars, a type of mandolin *(banduria)* and the *timple*, a small guitar with four strings that produces evocative samba-style rhythms. In between, resonant songs with a distinct Arabic influence and other lively ballads complete the repertoire. Rounds and other amusing dances are performed in groups, and some of the traditional sports are played out, much to the delight of the crowds. Activities include *lucha canaria*, a type of wrestling in which the object is to seize the turn-ups of the opponent's trousers and then floor him; *lucha de garrote*, a duel fought with sticks; *pulseo de piedra*, weight-lifting with lumps of rock and *salto del pastor*, in which shepherds jump across the *barrancos*.

Geological formation

According to geological research carried out on the bedrock, the Anaga mountains in the north-east, the area around Adeje in the southwest and the Teno hills in the northwest are made up of basalt that is older than the rest of the island. Scientists have therefore concluded that these three regions were originally separate islands, which were gradually fused into one larger volcanic island some 6000 m high. Further volcanic activity levelled off the summit at an altitude of 2000 m, thereby forming the present-day Cañadas crater, which measures around 45 km in circumference. Other volcanic eruptions at the island's northwestern edge created the Teide cone, partially covering the even older volcanic deposits of the Pico Viejo. The last volcanic eruption took place in 1909 when Chinyero, to the northwest of Teide, spewed lava for 10 consecutive days.

Guanches

Virtually no traces survive of the Guanches, the first inhabitants of the Canary Islands and Tenerife in particular; a few everyday objects and mummies are displayed in the museums and these artifacts consitute their only tangible remains. Many of the native islanders are proud of their Guanche roots, as this inheritance allows them to distance themselves from their Spanish conquerors. It is thought that there were two Guanche tribes: the Cro-magnons and the Mediterraneans. The former was characterized by a wide face with coarse features, while the latter had a longer face with more delicate features. At that time no links existed between the various islands, as maritime transport was unknown. The Guanches were peace-loving people with many positive characteristics. Their king on Tenerife was referred to as the Mencey. The death penalty was non-existent; however, thieves were severely punished and a beating was meted out to anyone who behaved disrespectfully toward women. Murderers were deprived of their possessions, which were given to the relatives of the victim as compensation. The local economy was based on breeding cattle and cultivating crops, and local artisans used clay to make pottery and handsome, handpainted utensils. Dwellings were either caves or stone huts roofed with straw. Clothes were prepared from tanned goat or sheepskin, while cheese, meat from goats or sheep, and gofio, roasted barley or wheat flour, were the staple foods, though they also ate fruit and fish, which were caught in nets woven from rushes or palm leaves. The Guanches were a monogamous people; marriage required the agreement of both partners, but could be dissolved at the request of either party. They believed in the existence of a higher being known as Aborac or Acoran. The dead were embalmed. Close examination of their language, customs, food and facial features points to a link with the Berbers. Anthropologists have therefore concluded that the Guanches probably arrived on the Canaries from Barbery, in present-day Libya. How they arrived remains a mystery.

Handicrafts

For many village families, handmade items are the only source of income. Standing on the outside, it can be difficult to identify small family-run businesses, but you only need to peek through the windows and doors of these old houses. Goods are often made for the larger companies that supply the tourist shops with these rustic products. Typical hand-made goods include tablecloths or materials edged with the traditional Canarian hemstitch, crochet-work, musical instruments, knives with ornate handles, embroidery, pottery and engraved jewellery. Often the goods that have not been bought by the wholesaler are sold direct to the tourists by the craftsmen themselves. In the remote rural areas, it is quite common to find women selling their modest wares from roadside stands. To haggle over prices in these circumstances would not really be fair. Many of these home-based artisans gather at the *feria*, a sort of craft fair, and sell the fruits of their labours directly to the tourists. Every area on the island has its own speciality. La Orotava, Los Realejos, La Guancha, San Juan de la Rambla and Granadilla are noted for their *calados*, hemstitch embroidery. Tablecloths, place-mats and napkins, and blouses are often decorated with this characteristic needlework. In La Guancha and the area around Buenavista and Masca, woven baskets and straw hats are produced. A straw cord is wrapped with soft thread, wool, raffia or hemp. The cord is then wound into a spiral and sewn together. Companies in La Orotava and Los Realejos specialize in making large baskets for shops. Bird cages made from bamboo canes are found in San Andrés and Icod de los Vinos, as is traditional pottery

made in the Guanche style (ie without a potter's wheel), including vases, ashtrays and jewellery boxes. Pottery studios are found in Los Cristianos, La Orotava and Güímar. The Canarios are skilled woodcarvers and the craftsmen in Buenavista, La Orotava and La Laguna in particular enjoy a good reputation. Musical instruments, such as the four-stringed *timple*, are made in Taganana and San Andrés. Local craftspeople also turn out handsome plates, cutlery, garlic mortars and cheese slices carved out of wood. Traditional Canarian wine presses and mini-balconies are produced in La Orotava and Los Realejos.

Lucha Canaria

Canarian wrestling is a very popular event among the locals, and some contests are even broadcast on regional television. This sport probably has its roots in a contest played out by the Guanches. Unlike conventional wrestling, it is not a game for two, rather it is a team sport with 12 players on each side and each team representing a district, village or island. Wrestlers are garbed in a shirt and a pair of trousers made from coarse linen. The trouser-legs, which are rolled up as high as possible on the thighs, play an important part in the game: opponents may grasp only this item of clothing and the player who manages to knock over an opponent within the ring wins a point. Anyone watching a contest for the first time might easily get the (mistaken) impression that the game consists of 24 athletes trying to pull each other's trousers off! But Canarian wrestling requires great physical strength and quick reflexes. As with Judo, the status of the wrestler is apparent from the colour of his belt. Beginners wear white belts, followed by yellow, orange, green, black, red and blue.

Tinerfeños

The population of Tenerife is mostly comprised of farming and fishing families, who have been hard hit by unemployment in recent years. Under Franco, state education was badly neglected and so illiteracy is not uncommon among the older generations. Only after democracy returned in the 1970s was compulsory education taken seriously. The inhabitants of Tenerife, known as *Tinerfeños,* today number around 600 000, which is approximately 287 people per square kilometre. They speak a dialect of Spanish, but with a strong south American influence. Particularly noticeable in their form of speech is the dropping of the letter 's' and word endings that are not fully articulated. *Tinerfeños* jokingly describe themselves as *chicharreros* after the chicharro fish.

It is generally true that the Tenerife islanders are a proud people, and they place a high value on appearances and giving a good impression to outsiders. Very Mediterranean in spirit, they interact with warmth and vivacity, though certain Latin behavioural clichés do prevail. Machismo still reigns among men. Tourism, however, has precipitated the emancipation of women, who now participate fully in running the community, notably being employed in the tourism and public administration sectors. In fact, the majority of students at La Laguna University today are women.

Young people delight in making noise – the louder the high-pitched whine of their mopeds, the better. At fiesta time, the volume control is usually set to high and the music carries on until early morning – as do the firecrackers, fireworks and gun salutes. Some outsiders who know the people well complain that *Tinerfeños* are selfish and live only for the moment, and that their charm is just a cover for insecurity. Tourists usually see the helpful and friendly side, but it is inadvisable to put too many demands on them. Visitors may find themselves being cold-shouldered. But the locals do have a sense of humour and they laugh and sing a lot and, as a rule, take their Catholic faith very seriously.

Water resources

In order to reach the water-table and the island's precious water reserves, it has sometimes been necessary to cut kilometre-long shafts or *galerías* into the mountainsides. There are now over 1000 such shafts with only about 200 yielding any water. The water that is extracted in this way is channelled to the villages and then pumped to the banana plantations. The right to draw water is largely in the hands of private landowners who, in some cases, date their ancestry back to the Spanish conquest, when the land was apportioned among the island's first settlers. Reserves are also stored in the *presas,* large open basins into which flow rainwater and excess water from the *galerías.*

Wildlife

The native fauna is markedly less varied than the flora. Only a few species of mammal live in the wild on Tenerife – rabbits, *moufflons* (a type of wild sheep introduced by hunters during the 1970s), wild cats, bats and hedgehogs. A wide variety of bird species, however, thrive on the Canary Islands. Some only congregate on the western islands, while others are confined to just one island. The blue Teide finch, a type of woodpecker (*picapinos*) and one particular species of robin breed only on Tenerife. Other indigenous birds include the peregrine falcon, golden eagle, wild pigeon, raven and the most infamous Canarian bird, the grey-green, rather unspectacular Canary finch. The bright yellow cage bird that we refer to as the canary was bred from the Canary finch. One or two migratory birds also winter on the island.

There are two reptile groups that inhabit the island: lizards and skinks. One type of lizard, dark in colour with greenish markings on its back, is endemic. The small gecko, which has small suction pads on its toes, can often be seen clinging to ceilings and is regarded by the locals as a harbinger of good luck. The skink, a small, smooth-skinned lizard, is olive-green on top with black sides. Small, light-green tree frogs can often be heard croaking in the evenings.

Beetles, cockroaches and butterflies represent the insect world, along with some species of spider. Beautifully coloured butterflies, some with a wing span stretching to 10 cm, flit from bloom to bloom. There are no scorpions or poisonous snakes on Tenerife. The only noxious creatures on the island are the mosquitoes.

The waters around Tenerife are replete with fish. *Viejas*, types of mullet that vary in colour from pink to silver grey, *salemas*, *chicharros*, sardines, *merluza* (hake), tuna, morays and many others can all be seen displayed on the fishmongers' slabs. There is also a wide variety of crustaceans and cephalopods, eg squid *(calamares)*, octopus *(pulpos)*, mussels *(mejillones)* and, of course, prawns and lobsters.

Landmarks

bay:	*bahía*	park:	*parque*
beach:	*playa*	peak:	*pico*
bridge:	*ponte*	plain:	*llanura*
cave/grotto:	*cueva*	port:	*puerto*
coast:	*costa*	river:	*rio*
cove:	*cala*	road:	*carretera*
field:	*campo*	rock:	*roque*
fountain:	*fuente*	scenery:	*paisaje*
gorge:	*barranco*	square:	*plaza*
meadow:	*prado*	view-point:	*mirador*
mountain:	*montaña, monte*	village:	*pueblo*

Canarian Cuisine

Hearty stews, home-grown vegetables and plenty of delicious fresh fish make for simple but very tasty local fare

Good, hearty food is fundamental to the Canarian way of life and Tinerfeños certainly know how to eat well. The local cuisine is simple and down-to-earth, both in preparation and in presentation, and is made with plenty of fresh, home-produced ingredients that guarantee flavourful results. Canarians don't stand on ceremony at the dinner table and those who are accustomed to swish foyers, expensive cutlery and liveried waiters will need to adjust to a different environment. The scene that unfolds behind a great portal may not be quite as grand as you anticipated; equally, a simple façade may conceal some very pleasant surprises.

Some of the best eateries are tucked away in the rural and coastal villages, where bars and restaurants are often little more than converted garages that could easily be overlooked by passing tourists. Of course, the main resorts and larger towns cater for a more international clientele and

A traditionally prepared Canarian fish dish, served with salt encrusted 'papas arrugadas'

it is possible to dine in a more European style. If you cannot survive without a full English breakfast, or roast beef and Yorkshire pudding at lunchtime, suitable restaurants abound. There are even a number of Chinese restaurants to satisfy cravings for prawn crackers and chow mein. But if you want to sample authentic Canarian cuisine, you need to venture beyond the boundaries of the tourist resorts.

A visit to a typical Canarian restaurant often proves to be more than just a culinary experience. Guests are generally seated in an open patio, surrounded by lush greenery and flowers, with perhaps a gently splashing fountain among them. The ceilings within are supported by thick, solid beams and the walls are used to display trinkets and old-fashioned cooking utensils. This is the classic type of restaurant you will come across in Puerto de la Cruz and the inland villages. But such establishments do not necessarily serve genuine Canarian food. The best way to find the real thing is to follow your nose. If you can detect the waft of braised meat, fish, herbs and, of course, garlic, then you are on the right track. Such mouth-watering smells emanate from guaranteed palate-pleasers, conjured up from the island's staple fare: fish and seafood, chicken, rabbit, potatoes and a variety of fresh vegetables.

Soup *(sopa)* – vegetable soup *(sopa de verdura)*, garlic soup *(sopa de ajo)*, or fish soup *(sopa de pescado)* made with a variety of seafood – is the classic starter, but grilled prawns served with a garlic dip is a popular alternative that is well worth trying. *Papas arrugadas* are a Canarian speciality and served practically everywhere. These small, wrinkled potatoes are served in a covered pot, having been steamed either in seawater or liberally salted tapwater until all the liquid has evaporated, leaving a crusty layer of dried salt on top of the potato skin which may be either eaten or discarded.

Garlic is a fundamental ingredient and is added liberally to meat and fish dishes, soups and, in particular, to the hot *mojo* sauce that accompanies most Canarian specialities. To make this red sauce, sea salt, hot paprika or chilli and garlic are crushed with a pestle and mortar, then mixed together thoroughly with vinegar and oil. It tastes a little bit like a spicy vinaigrette. *Mojo verde* is a 'green' variation, in which coriander or parsley is used as a substitute for paprika.

On excursions inland it is not unusual to hear the sound of gunshots ring out from the rifles of hunters out to catch wild rabbits *(conejos salvajes)*. In most tourist areas, however, the rabbit served in restaurants is domestically reared rather than wild. These *conejos mansos* are specially bred for the dinner plate. *Conejo salmorejo*, rabbit in a hot sauce, is the most popular rabbit dish. It is delicious with *papas arrugadas*, *patatas fritas* (chips) or *patatas sorpresa* (surprise potatoes).

Chicken is another favourite that is usually served from the spit, though it also comes braised. One tasty Canarian speciality is diced chicken that has been braised in a hot, rather oily sauce, served with *papas*. Another typical Canarian dish called *puchero* is made with a variety of meats, potatoes, vegetables, chick peas, and sometimes noodles, that are mixed together and slowly stewed in a large pot.

By far the most popular types of fish are *cherne*, a member of the sea bass family, *merluza* (hake) and *vieja*, the local name for parrotfish. Sole is often featured on menus, but it is usually imported frozen from more remote fishing grounds. If you want a really well-prepared and well-cooked sole, it is better to seek out a high-quality fish restaurant, as proper preparation is often skimped in the simpler, more basic establishments. On the other hand, shell fish caught in local waters is treated as a real delicacy, one that is greatly appreciated by the islanders themselves, who are experts in its preparation. Gourmets will relish the king prawns *(langostinos)*, prawns *(gambas)*, crabs *(cangrejos)* and various types of mussels and whelks *(lapas)*. Octopus *(pulpos)*, usually smallish varieties, are sliced into pieces, fried and served as *tapas*. Calamar or squid are served whole or else chopped into morsels, also as *tapas*.

Banana-based desserts are a common menu item. A favourite is flambéd banana sweetened with a liqueur and honey, although crème caramel *(tocino de cielo)* and almond tart *(tarta de almendras)* are also popular choices.

Tapas

Tapas can be served as hors d'oeuvres or as a main course, with several smaller portions combined to make a substantial meal. Usually, *tapas* are small plates filled with pieces of crispy sausage or meatballs in sauce, little herring fillets or tuna salad with a spicy seasoning. Another favourite is potato salad with finely-chopped eggs and fresh herbs. Most locals savour *tapas* as a mid-morning snack to fill the gap between breakfast and what many would regard as a late lunch, but often it's just a good excuse to disappear into a bar for a drink!

Cheese

Although Tenerife does not boast many well-known types of cheese such as those produced on the neighbouring islands of La Palma and Hierro, the Tinerfeños are real cheese fanatics. The white goats' cheese, *queso blanco*, is one home-produced speciality, but there are plenty of other Canarian cheeses available here, including a superbly flavoured smoked goats' cheese.

Wines

One hundred years ago, wine was one of Tenerife's main exports. Today, although production has tapered off, the quality has improved dramatically as small wine producers have invested in modern equipment to process the grape juice. Until recently, wine was sold in bars as a basic table wine, but many cellars now supply it in bottles endorsed with a seal of quality. The vintages of Tenerife have received numerous awards, with the reds from Tacoronte and the whites from Icod/La Guancha at the forefront. Red wines are produced mainly around Santa Úrsula, La Victoria, Tacoronte and La Matanza. White and rosé wines are predominantly from Icod de los Vinos, Los Realejos and La Guancha. As the local vineyards are a long way from meeting the demands of the hotels and restaurants, wines from the European mainland, and primarily those from Spain, are frequently featured on restaurant wine lists.

Other beverages

After breakfast, a rather modest meal by northern European standards, the bars fill up quickly. The most likely choice for the locals will be a *cortado*, an espresso coffee with condensed milk, or else a glass of red wine. Mineral water helps to quench a real thirst after exertions in the hot sun and this is bottled on the island at Vilaflor. *Coñac*, which is officially described as brandy, is also popular and there is usually a wide choice of brands and flavours on offer. Wine is consumed in large quantities and at any time of day, while you can get cold beer on tap in most places. Bars in the main tourist resorts sell English, Dutch and German beers. In the evenings, many restaurants offer *sangría*, a type of punch based on red wine but mixed with other, stronger spirits – watch out, it is often deceptively strong. Order a *café solo* or a *cortado* if you want an espresso coffee. Filter coffee is often described as *café alemán* (German coffee).

Gofio

Gofio is to Canarians what flour is to north Europeans although the natives accord it a much higher status. The discovery of this staple food, which is made from roasted barley, wheat or maize flour, is attributed to the Guanches and it continues to be an important component of the local diet. Called *gofio* – meaning the 'bread of the poor' – by the Spanish conquistadors, it has no place on restaurant menus, although it is a very important item in the domestic larder. Many agricultural workers and shepherds still eat *gofio* to keep them going during the day. They carry a leather pouch *(zurrón)* made from goatskin, in which the *gofio* is prepared as required: flour is mixed with milk or water and, once it is well kneaded, bite-sized chunks are pulled from the dough and eaten. It may not be everyone's favourite daytime snack, but it is certainly one that is greatly appreciated by the local farm-workers.

Mealtimes

The Canarians love to eat, especially in the company of family, friends and acquaintances. Mealtimes are lively, informal social occasions that are never hurried. Breakfast *(desayuno)* is fairly standard and simple, consisting mainly of coffee with milk *(café con leche)* or a small, strong espresso, taken either black *(café solo)* or with a dash of milk *(café cortado)*, a sandwich or *bocadillo*, a white roll with a sweet filling, such as jam or honey, or a thick wedge of ham, cheese or *chorizo*, the much-loved Spanish spicy sausage. In contrast to most European eating habits, the Tinerfeños take their main meals late. Lunch *(almuerzo)* is rarely eaten before 2 pm and families don't usually gather for the evening meal *(cena)* before 8 or 9 pm. As

Dining 'al fresco' in Adeje

supper is served quite late, it's not unusual to have a late afternoon snack, usually a sandwich (*merienda*) to fill the gap. For many Canarians, eating is an extended ritual especially at weekends when the village restaurants fill up with local people and the gathering is usually a lively one. Everyone enjoys their food and the noisy chatter continues until late. Bones accumulate on the table and left-overs are fed to the dogs. Some people may turn up their noses at the apparent lack of hygiene but, for Canarians, if a meal is to be fully appreciated, there must be plenty of food to go round.

In many of the restaurants along the coast, guests are invited to select their own fish directly from the kitchen. The price is then determined by its weight. Side dishes such as potatoes and salads are charged separately. One habit that restaurateurs in Tenerife have adopted is to put bread and butter on the table before the main course arrives. The cost of this starter (usually between 25p and 75p) is then added to the bill whether it is eaten or not. If you do not want this additional item, then you should hand it back as soon as it is placed on the table.

Restaurant categories

There are various categories of restaurant on Tenerife, but the official classification system that uses a scale of forks (1-5) is rather arbitrary as it doesn't seem to reflect accurately the quality of the food or service. Most restaurants in the Canaries are described as *Bar/Restaurante* and are a combination of a restaurant, wine bar and pub. They offer both à la carte and set menus. Away from the tourist resorts, many establishments refer to themselves simply as a *Bar*, although they frequently serve full meals. *Bodegas* are specifically wine bars, often in a cellar-style setting. Many villages have corner shops or *ventas* that double as bars. The prices here are often surprisingly low.

A selection of restaurants is given for each town or village mentioned in this guide.

What's on the menu?

beer:	cerveza	ice-cream:	helado
the bill:	la cuenta	knife:	cuchillo
bread:	pan	meat:	carne
butter:	mantequilla	menu:	lista, menú
cheese:	queso	omelette:	tortilla
chips:	patatas fritas	rice:	arroz
dessert:	postre	salad:	ensalada
dish:	plato	steak:	filete
fish:	pescado	vegetables:	legumbres
fork:	tenedor	waiter:	camarero
glass:	vaso	water:	aqua
ham:	jamón	wine:	vino

Verde

HANDICRAFT
ARTESANIA CANARI

Woodcarvers and lacemakers

Markets in the towns and villages regale the senses with colourful sights and mouth-watering smells

Take a quick stroll down the main shopping street when you arrive and it will be apparent after only a few glances that Tenerife has plenty to offer the dedicated shopper. Pedestrian zones and shopping malls are crammed with boutiques, and the atmosphere is not unlike that of an Eastern bazaar. Many of the shops are run by industrious Indians whose shelves are piled high with goods from all over the world, including boxes of transistor radios, videos, cassette recorders and mini-TV sets from the Far East. Electric razors and household appliances made in Hong Kong are sold at bargain prices. Jewellery shop windows gleam with jade and ivory, semi-precious stones and sparkling rings, pearls and chains in gold and silver. You will also find watches, pens, suitcases, cashmere jumpers, etc. An amazing variety of junk souvenirs and odds and ends of questionable value overflow from the bargain boxes

*Arts and crafts for sale
Playa de las Américas*

placed at shop entrances to draw the customers in. If you like Oriental style shopping and want to haggle, the traders here will be happy to oblige.

If you're looking for quality and authenticity, however, then it is better to seek out the specialist shops, where the staff usually speak good English. When buying jewellery, clocks or photographic equipment don't be tempted by suspiciously good bargains. The quality is nearly always reflected in the price.

It is now virtually impossible to find genuine antiques, even though you may see plenty to interest you. The objects on sale are more than likely to be new, but given an antique finish for an old-world look.

There is plenty on offer for modern art lovers, who stand a good chance of picking up a memorable keepsake from one of the many art galleries and shops that sell oil paintings, prints and reproductions.

A number of resorts boast modern multi-storey shopping centres. These labyrinthine complexes house everything from luxury boutiques selling the latest fashions, high-class jewellers and accessory shops to bazaars, bars, cafés and restaurants. The atmosphere in these consumer havens hovers between that of a supermarket, a games hall and a dealing room. Customers rummage, fumble and snatch until they fall upon the perfect outfit for the beach or night-club. Around the corner teenagers try on unlabelled jeans at bargain prices. The innumerable types of perfume and cosmetics are hard to resist, especially as all the well-known brands are readily available and the prices rarely matched even by the duty-free shops at the airport.

Rebajas are end-of-season sales and a sign saying *liquidación total* indicates a closing-down sale; both are worth investigating for bargains. Many shops claim to have *rebajas* all year round and prices here are genuinely rock-bottom. Alcohol and cigarettes are remarkably cheap wherever you buy them but are especially good value in supermarkets.

Leather goods from Spain or Africa are popular souvenirs while hand-made products from the Canary Islands in general and Tenerife in particular make more conventional souvenirs. Tenerife is renowned for its craft industry. Pottery, woodcarvings and straw or cane basketware are skilfully and painstakingly produced by craftsmen, either in their own homes or in small workshops. Canarian embroidery, particularly the open threadwork pieces from Tenerife, is of outstanding quality. With this type of sewing, the material is partially unravelled and then, with a special hemstitching technique, patterns

Tenerife lace in the making

and motifs such as suns and roses, are stitched on. The production of these filigree patterns has become a real art form on the island and the observant visitor will spot a variety of motifs embroidered on table-cloths, table-mats and handkerchiefs. The lace from Vilaflor and La Palma, which has been made by the same family for over 50 years, is reputed to be among the best. Sadly this is a dying art as fewer and fewer women are carrying on the tradition.

To truly indulge all the senses, a visit to at least one of the outdoor markets is a must. Everything that nature has bestowed on this island in such abundance is displayed here in all its colourful glory. Traders peddle their wares competing for custom with booming voices. Fruit, vegetables, flowers and house plants spill over heavily laden stalls. The perfume of oriental spices, fish stalls and the musty odour of fresh seaweed combines with the earthy pungency of live chickens, rabbits and ducks to create an aromatic blend that rewards passersby (provided they can overcome their inhibitions) with a veritable symphony for the nose.

Carpets of flowers

With festivals and carnivals all year round, the inhabitants of Tenerife certainly know how to celebrate

The following days are public holidays and offices, post offices and banks will be closed. However, many towns have their own individual festivals, usually the patron saint's day, in which case closures only apply locally.

HOLIDAYS & FESTIVALS

January

1 January: *Año Nuevo*, New Year's Day

6 January: *Los Reyes Magos*, Epiphany, when children are given presents; on the previous day the three ·kings parade through town

22 January: *Fiesta de San Sebastián*, the Feast of San Sebastian, the patron saint of Garachico and Los Realejos

Beginning of January to mid-February: ★ *Canary Island Music Festival*; classical music in Santa Cruz and La Orotava

February

2 February: *Candelaria*, Candlemas; patronal festival in Candelaria

February/March: ★ *Carnival*. Processions, flamboyant costumes, music and dancing in the streets and squares throughout the island. The highlights are the crowning of the carnival queen in Santa Cruz and the 'Burial of the Sardine'.

March/April

2 March: *Fiesta de San Benito Abad*, Feast of St Benedict in La Laguna

March/April: *Semana Santa,* Holy Week. All the holy statues are taken from inside the churches and paraded through the streets. The ★ Holy Week processions in Santa Cruz and La Laguna are probably the most impressive.

March/April: *Pascua*, Easter

May/June

1 May: *Día del Trabajo*, Labour Day; beginning of the May festivals. Flower display in Santa Cruz

3 May: *Día de la Cruz*, Feast of the Cross, holidays in all places which bear the name 'Cruz'. Religious processions in which locals carry a cross. All over the island, crosses are decorated with flowers and firework displays are held.

May/June: *Pentecostés*, Whitsun

May/June: *Corpus Christi*. Solemn processions throughout the

island. La Orotava and La Laguna are the best places to see the ★ ornate pavement tableaux designed with freshly cut flowers (see page 15).
30 May: *Día de Canarias*, Canary Island Day

July

2nd Sunday after Corpus Christi (June/July): ★ *Romería de San Isidro*; revellers in La Orotava parade through the streets in brightly-coloured costumes.
1st Sunday in July: *Fiesta y Romería de San Benito Abad*, Feast of St Benedict and pilgrimage in La Laguna.
16 July: ★ *Fiesta de la Virgen del Carmen y del Gran Poder* in Puerto de la Cruz. Feast of the patron saint with procession of fishing boats off the coast. The festivities, which are centred around the old town and the Plaza del Charco, last almost the whole of July.
25 July: *Fiesta de Santiago Apóstol*,

A folk group in traditional costume plays some island music

Feast of St James, the patron saint of Spain.

August

15 August: *Asunción de María*, Assumption. ★ *Romería de la Virgen de Candelaria*; pilgrims from all over the island come to Candelaria to honour the patroness of the archipelago.
3rd Sunday in August: *Fiesta de Cristo del Gran Poder* in Bajamar

September

7-21 September: *Fiesta del Santísimo* in La Laguna and Tacoronte

October

5 October: *Fiesta de la Misericordia* in Garachico
12 October: *Día de la Hispanidad*, *Fiesta de Nuestra Señora del Pilar*

December

6 December: *Día de la Constitución*, Constitution Day and a national holiday
8 December: *Inmaculada Concepción*, Immaculate Conception
25 December: *Navidad del Señor*, Christmas Day

MARCO POLO SELECTION: FESTIVALS

1 Carnival
Spectacular carnival festivities in every town and village (page 31)

2 Semana Santa
Grand carnival processions in Santa Cruz and La Laguna (page 31)

3 Corpus Christi
Ornate carpets of flowers in La Orotava and La Laguna (page 33)

4 Romería de San Isidro
Harvest thanksgiving in La Orotava (page 33)

5 Fiestas de Julio
Boat procession in Puerto de la Cruz (page 33)

6 Romería de la Virgen de Candelaria
Festival of the Virgin Mary lasting several days (page 33)

7 Canary Island Music Festival
Classical music in Santa Cruz and La Orotava (page 31)

Paradise on earth

Historic towns and charming fishing villages nestle among banana plantations and vineyards

The stretch of motorway that hugs the coastline along the 5 km-wide Orotava valley is quite breathtaking offering wonderful views of the sea beyond a steeply sloping verdant landscape. Banana plantations are everywhere, interspersed with the occasional palm tree, brightly coloured flowers and gleaming white villages. Standing guard over it all is Teide, with its bright cone-

Seawater swimming pool in a Puerto de la Cruz hotel

shaped peak. Towering hotel blocks line the lower coastal stretch beside Puerto de la Cruz. The 100 m high Tigaiga precipice rises out of the western end of the valley; beyond, a sheer rocky ridge extends as far as Garachico. The lower region is barren and rocky, while the higher, more fertile land is worked by the local inhabitants. Pine forests and terraced fields, where potatoes and vines are cultivated, characterize the sloping landscape. The Isla Baja beyond Garachico is much flatter, and oranges and bananas

---

Hotel and Restaurant Prices

Hotels
Category 1: 20 000-25 000 ptas
Category 2: 13 500-18 500 ptas
Category 3: 9500-13 000 ptas
These prices are for a double room (two people), including breakfast. Many hotels have up to four seasonal price ranges.

Restaurants
Category 1: 2000-2500 ptas

Category 2: 1100-2000 ptas
Category 3: 950-1100 ptas
Prices per person for a main meal.

Abbreviations
Avda.	*Avenida*	Avenue
C/.	*Calle*	Road
Ctra.	*Carretera*	Main road
Edf.	*Edificio*	Building
ptas	*Pesetas*	Pesetas
Urb.	*Urbaniza-ción*	Holiday village

are grown here. To the south of the Isla Baja, the steep Teno hills rise up and then continue on toward the sea behind Buenavista. At the western tip, Punta de Teno is ringed by a small, isolated plain and it's a tortuous route southward from here across the 1000 m-high Teno hills, which are scored by deep gorges and steep precipices. Small, impoverished villages nestle in the valleys, surrounded by leafy vegetation. Laurels and tree heath woods alternate with cultivated strips and palm tree groves.

LA OROTAVA

(C3) Sturdy shoes and a strong pair of legs are required for the steep streets of this picturesque town (pop. 36 000). Cobbled roads wend their way along the sheer slopes of the western Orotava valley. Old churches, monasteries and palaces testify to the wealth that the fertile valley bestowed on the Spanish colonists. Many of the houses, with their ornately carved shutters, balconies and oriel windows, date from the 17th and 18th centuries.

La Orotava is divided by the Barranco Araujo, a gorge which cuts down between the houses towards the valley. At the heart of the town lies the Plaza de la Constitución, which crosses the Barranco Araujo on a two-level platform. This square is sometimes referred to as the 'balcony of La Orotava' because of the stunning panorama it offers over the rooftops and right across to the sea. To the north-east of the square stands the church and former cloisters of San Agustín, now a barracks.

Founded during the early colonial era at the beginning of the 16th century, the town quickly grew into an influential and prosperous settlement. Today, La Orotava remains an important business, administrative and educational centre that is largely untouched by the advent of tourism.

SIGHTS

Botanical Garden

This small park lies behind the town hall, and is an annex of the renowned botanical garden situated between Puerto de la Cruz and La Orotava. It is home to an interesting variety of tropical plants from Australia, Malaysia, South America and India.

Casas de los Balcones

★ Of all the balcony houses in Calle San Francisco, which are distinctive for their beautifully sculpted verandas and inner courtyards, no. 4 is the most striking. This grand mansion dates from the mid-17th century and now houses an embroidery school. Hand-made crafts and other souvenirs are available here. *C/. San Francisco*

Convento Molina

↘↗ Crafts, pictures and other gifts and souvenirs are also on sale in this old convent (1590). The flower-carpeted balcony offers a fine view over the valley. *C/. San Francisco*

Gofio mill

Gofio is still milled here. One room is reserved for roasting the barley and another for grinding. Old photographs displayed on the walls show how the mill

functioned in the days before electricity, when the wheel was turned by a stream that flowed through the street (in which women did their washing). Some way up the steep lane, the remains of two other abandoned mills can still be seen.
C/. Dr Domingo González

Hospital de la Santísima Trinidad and the Church of San Francisco

Displayed in the entrance to the hospital is an interesting contraption that provided an early solution to the problem of giving up unwanted children. A revolving cradle with a straw cushion was used in order to maintain the anonymity of unfortunate mothers who had to give up their children; the cradle was only turned inwards when the mother had left and the baby had started to cry. The child was then taken into the convent where it was raised.
C/. San Francisco

The Church of Nuestra Señora de la Concepción

★ The finest Baroque church on the island (18th-century). A large, self-supporting dome with a smaller dome on top gives the central nave area a feeling of height. At the side altars stand statues of the Mater Dolorosa and St John by Luján Pérez. The marble high altar and pulpit are the work of Italian artists.
Plaza Casañas

MARCO POLO SELECTION: THE NORTH-WEST COAST

1 Aguamansa
Popular walking area amid the pine forests, 1000 m above sea level (page 45)

2 Casas de los Balcones
A typical Canarian balcony house in La Orotava's Calle San Francisco, now home to an embroidery school (page 36)

3 Playa Jardín
A new 'garden' beach in Puerto de la Cruz, designed by the brilliant architect César Manrique (page 44)

4 Dragon tree
A symbol for the island in Icod de los Vinos (page 47)

5 Nuestra Señora de la Concepción
An interesting church in La Orotava (page 37)

6 Las Arenas Negras
Area above Garachico, popular with walkers who want to explore the island's youngest volcano (page 47)

7 Loro Parque
Zoo and shows in Puerto de la Cruz (page 41)

8 Masca
A remote village in a gorge at the heart of the Teno hills (page 48)

9 Punta de Teno
A lonely coastal region with a lighthouse (page 48)

Liceo de Taoro

Now a small private club, this palace is sometimes used to stage cultural events.
Plaza de la Constitución

RESTAURANTS

Café Taoro

A popular café with the locals, renowned for its selection of delicious cakes.
Daily 10.00-20.00 hrs; C/. Léon 5

El Engazo

This restaurant occupies an old house decorated in rustic style. Rabbit a speciality.
Daily (except Tuesday) 13.00-16.00 and 19.00-24.00 hrs; Situated in La Luz district behind the pottery museum; Category 3

Las Caseosas

Canarian specialities in an old mansion with a pretty patio.
Daily 10.00-24.00 hrs; La Carrera 21, below the Casas de los Balcones; Category 2

SHOPPING

La Orotava is the best place to buy *calados*, 'open threadwork' embroidery, but nice hand-woven baskets in all shapes and sizes, and woodcarvings, can also be found here.

Artesanía Balcón Canario

Well-stocked souvenir shop with plenty of hand-made goods.
C/. Viera 23,25

Casa de los Balcones

Tablecloths, napkins, blouses and many other items, all with hand-embroidered decorations.
C/. San Francisco 4

Convento Molino

Offers a similar selection of souvenirs to Casa de los Balcones, but also has a picture gallery.
C/. San Francisco 5

Centro Comercial

Multi-storey shopping complex by the bus station. Rows of small shops selling everyday items.
Avenida Benítez de Lugo

HOTELS

La Orotava is poorly supplied with hotels. There is just one pension:

Silene

Old-fashioned rooms may be had for 2200 ptas per person.
C/. Tomás Zerolo 9; Tel: 33 01 99, 33 14 80

INFORMATION

Ayuntamiento

Daily 10.00-14.00 hrs; Carrera del Escultor Estévez; Tel: 33 00 50, Fax: 33 39 11

PUERTO DE LA CRUZ

(**C3**) Situated at the far end of the Orotava Valley, this fishing port has rapidly become the biggest tourist resort on the island. The numerous leisure activities on offer make it an ideal holiday destination. However, the skies are not always guaranteed to be blue as they are often covered with a thick blanket of cloud, especially in winter.

Puerto de la Cruz lies a good hour's drive away from the southern airport. The town centre (pop. 27 000) is situated beyond the Botanical Gardens and the peaceful, up-market La Paz district, where tourists stroll among the terraced cafés. A 50 m high cliff separates this quarter of the town from the old central area beneath. Down below, the Atlantic waves wash up towards the grey hotel blocks so hurriedly erected in the 1960s when the tourist boom got underway. A promenade runs from La Paz, beside the sea, past the seawater swimming pools, across Calle de San Telmo and into the well-preserved town centre.

Puerto de la Cruz originated as a port for La Orotava to facilitate the export of produce from the valley and, in the early days, numerous English and Portuguese traders settled here. Their prosperity led to the construction of some splendid houses and the town soon began to develop its own cultural scene. These grand old town houses have now been turned into hotels, restaurants and shops.

At the heart of the old town lies the recently altered Plaza del Charco which is shaded by a cluster of mature trees. Locals and tourists congregate around the comfortable, terraced cafés, tended by scurrying waiters who never seem to stop for breath. Shoeshine boys and lottery ticket and newspaper salesmen mill among the clientele. During carnival and fiesta time, this is the hub of the fun and celebrations.

The nearby harbour also hums with activity, especially in the early hours when the fishermen disembark to unload their catch, which goes straight from the boat to the fishstall.

During the winter months, high Atlantic waves surge toward the black lava coastline and it is often too dangerous to swim in the surf. But swimmers can enjoy the seawater pool whatever the weather. Playa Jardín in the Punta Brava district is a new beach with fine black sand and some attractive lawns, bars, restaurants and facilities.

SIGHTS & MUSEUMS

Archaeological Museum
This interesting collection gives a moving account of the island's history.
In the old town pedestrian zone, C/. del Lomo 9A; Tues-Sat 09.00-13.00 and 17.00-21.00 hrs, Sunday 09.00-13.00 hrs

Bananera El Guanche
Model banana plantation with souvenir shop.
Daily 09.30-17.45 hrs; On the main road towards the motorway, free bus every 20 minutes; Entrance 750 ptas

Botanical Gardens
The idea of a botanical garden originated in 1778 during the reign of Carlos III. Experiments were carried out here on cotton and tobacco plants, both of which thrived in the mild climate. Tropical plants from all over the world were brought here in order to acclimatize them to a more European climate. The garden's main patron was the Marqués de Villanueva del Prado, who had a hill cleared near El Durazno and began planting in 1795. The climate turned out to be ideal and some fine examples of the plants that were cultivated then still exist.
Daily 09.00-18.00 hrs; Ctra. del Botánico, La Paz; Entrance 100 ptas

Casa Iriarte

The birthplace of Tomás de Iriarte now houses a maritime museum. Models of ships from all over the world are displayed in the large rooms on the first floor of this patrician mansion, while on the ground floor Canarian embroidery is sold.

Daily (except Sunday and public holidays) 09.00-19.00 hrs; Corner of C/. San Juan and C/. Iriarte; Entrance 200 ptas

Castillo de San Felipe

This seaside fortress at the western end of the town was built at the beginning of the 17th century. It is now used for exhibitions and cultural events.

Paseo Luis Lavaggi

Fishing port

By the turn of the 19th century there were several working ports in Puerto de la Cruz: two for merchant shipping and a number of smaller fishing harbours. The biggest harbour, the Puerto Viejo, lay to the west of Castillo de San Felipe. At that time, the Barranco San Felipe widened out into a bay where boats could moor, but this natural port was destroyed during a storm in 1826. All that remains are the two jetties of La Caleta harbour and these are used only by a few fishing boats. The 500 m sea wall that stretches to the east protects the harbour from the crashing Atlantic breakers and the ocean swell. From here, there is a splendid view of the old town and the mountainous backdrop.

Hotel Marquesa

This building was once the property of the Irish Cologan family who ran a trading centre here.

Among the illustrious guests who stayed here were Captain Cook and Alexander von Humboldt. It was eventually converted into a hotel in 1820.

C/. Quintana 11

Old Customs House

This traditional Canarian house was built back in 1620 by the founder of the harbour, Don Juan de Franchi. When Garachico harbour was destroyed, the customs officials of the Royal Treasury moved here. The house itself is now privately owned and no longer open to the public, but there is a souvenir and embroidery shop on the ground floor. It has a splendid interior courtyard.

C/. Lonjas

San Amaro chapel

The aristocratic Candia family from La Orotava worshipped San Amaro as their patron saint and protector. In 1596 they built a small chapel in his honour on the cliff above Puerto de la Cruz. Years later, the Irishman Walsh-Valois acquired the site and named it La Paz to symbolize his strong yearning for peace. A platform opposite the chapel provides a fine view of the town below. On the right, a flight of steps leads up to a promenade with a café.

At the end of Camino San Amaro

San Telmo chapel

This chapel was founded by mariners in 1780 to honour their patron saint San Pedro González Telmo. The square around the chapel was once occupied by a fortress of the same name. The surviving wash-houses and wooden palisades were once part

Dolphins in the Loro Parque

of the fortifications.
C/. San Telmo, currently undergoing restoration

Pottery museum

Pieces of pottery have been gathered from all over Spain and are displayed in this 16th-century feudal manor. Adjacent to the collections are a pottery studio and shop.
Daily 10.00-16.45 hrs; La Candia district; Hourly bus service; Entrance 350 ptas

Church of Nuestra Señora de la Peña de Francia

The present church was constructed between 1684 and 1697, but the Baroque tower wasn't added until 1898. Of artistic interest are the pulpit, which was painted by de la Cruz y Ríos, and the altar figures by Estévez and Luján Pérez. The square outside is lined with palm trees and flower beds, and features a 'swan' fountain.

PLEASURE PARKS

Free buses to the various pleasure parks leave from opposite the Café Columbus in Avenida Colón.

Lago de Martiánez

Large seawater swimming pool with islands and waterways.
Avda. Colón; Entrance for adults: 335 ptas, for children: 170 ptas

Loro Parque

★ Loro Parque is the main tourist attraction on the island and boasts the biggest collection of parrots in the world. Visitors are also entertained with dolphin, sea-lion and parrot shows. Recent additions include an 18 m shark tunnel, a Thai village, a bat cave and a gorilla enclosure. At lunchtime, visitors can choose between a number of picnic areas, a café-restaurant and a self-service restaurant. The bus service has been replaced by a miniature railway that you can pick up opposite the Café Columbus.
Daily 08.30-17.00 hrs; In the Punta Brava district; Entrance for adults: 2300 ptas, for children: 1150 ptas, and special prices for groups

Risco Bello

The moment you set foot in this park you will be overcome by a feeling of total relaxation and idleness. Sit down and enjoy the spacious lawns and gardens, which are planted with Canarian trees, shrubs and flowers. A café in the middle of the park is the perfect place for a refreshing drink.
Daily 11.00-21.00 hrs; Near the Casino Taoro

Taoropark

The town's greenery extends down the hillside in stages. This flower-filled park is another haven. It's hard to resist lingering on the park benches or under the shade of the old trees. Footpaths run alongside a waterfall, and there is a viewing platform ∿⁄▹ that provides a marvellous panorama of the town and coastline. There is also a children's play area.

RESTAURANTS

La Bodeguita
Down-to-earth restaurant serves wine from the barrel, ham and tapas.
Open all day; Plaza de Europa, opposite the town hall; Category 3

La Boheme
Quality restaurant, elegantly appointed. Speciality dishes.
Daily; Near the Plaza del Charco; C/. Blanco 5, 1st floor; Category 1

La Papaya
Typical Canarian restaurant serving traditional fare. Lovely patio with fountain and luxuriant flowers and foliage.
Daily (except Monday) 12.00-15.00 and 18.00-23.00 hrs; C/. del Lomo 10; Category 2

Régulo
This well-run establishment is located in a traditional Canarian house in the old town with small, comfortable and elegantly-decorated rooms. In addition to the usual Canarian cuisine, provincial Spanish specialities are served.
Daily 12.00-15.00 and 18.00-23.00 hrs; C/. San Felipe; Category 2

Taoro
∿⁄▹ Offers one of the finest views in Puerto de la Cruz. Traditional Canarian cuisine. Fresh fish and rabbit on the menu every day.
Open all day; In the Taoropark, below the Casino Taoro; Category 2

SHOPPING

Arte Ponsjoan
Oil paintings of local landscape and island themes, for purchase directly from the artist.
C/. Quintana

Galerie Colombe
Prints, lithographs, etchings, oil paintings and exhibitions.
In the Canary Shopping Centre, La Paz

Karinias silkpainting
Delicate hand-painted scarves, blouses and other fashion items produced in the workshop from real silk.
Sat/Sun 10.00-13.00 hrs; La Paz, C/. Aceviño 45

Lladró
Large selection of Spanish porcelain.
Plaza San Telmo

Martiánez Center
This modern shopping complex is spread over two storeys and makes for an inviting place to shop or just to stroll through. Many elegant stores and boutiques sell a wide selection of goods. The complex also includes a large supermarket, bars, cafés and a small fun fair for children. Underground car-park.
Daily 10.00-21.00 hrs; Beneath the San Felipe Hotel

Mercado San Felipe
A modern covered market-hall selling fruit, vegetables, meat and fish. The various shops are spread over three storeys.
Daily 09.00-13.00 hrs and 16.00-19.00 hrs; Avda. Blas Pérez Gonzales, at the western end of the town

Shopping Center Columbus

A Canarian-style complex close to the Plaza del Charco. Several restaurants as well as a string of attractive shops.
Daily 09.00-20.00 hrs

Visanta

Bazaar selling electronic novelty items.
Avda. General Franco

HOTELS

Many of the hotels in Puerto de la Cruz were built in the 1960s when the tourist boom was getting underway and most of them are close to the town centre. It wasn't long before there was no space left to build in and around the town centre, and so developers turned to neighbouring areas such as the district of La Paz. The advantage of the newer hotels is that they are situated in a quieter and more attractive area, although they are quite a long way from the beach and the town centre. All hotels have swimming pools and shuttle-bus service into town.

Don Manolito

A hotel on the edge of the town centre about a five-minute walk from Punta Brava. It is a family-run establishment with a friendly and informal atmosphere. All 49 rooms are well furnished, with balconies. Facilities include swimming pool, sun terrace, bar, lounge with TV.
C/. Dr Madan; Tel: 38 50 12, Fax: 37 08 77; Category 3

Hotel/Apartamentos Maritim

This hotel and apartment block lies behind the Punta Brava district in an extremely quiet location beside the sea. The rooms are spacious and comfortably furnished. It features two swimming pools and several sun terraces. Plenty of sport and leisure activities laid on, including an in-house disco. Hotel-owned buses.
451 rooms, Burgado, Los Realejos; Tel: 34 20 12, Fax: 34 21 06; Category 1

Meliá Botánico

Five-star luxury hotel with a superb garden and suites with private pool. Every possible amenity to match its rating.
282 rooms; opposite the Botanical Garden; Tel: 38 14 00, Fax: 38 15 04; Category 1

Prinsotel La Chiripa Garden

A holiday complex in a quiet part of the town on the edge of the Taoro park. Hidden away in a vast (30 000 sq m) well-tended palm garden, it has two swimming pools, several sun terraces, two pool bars and a café-restaurant, a lounge with satellite TV and a wide choice of sport and entertainment facilities, so there is no chance of boredom setting in. There is even a health and fitness centre. The atmosphere is relaxed and very friendly.
362 rooms; Urb. San Fernando; Tel: 38 20 50, Fax: 38 08 93; Category 1

Pensión Rosa Mari

Simple but comfortable rooms. Double room for 2500 ptas.
C/. San Felipe; Tel: 38 32 53

Tigaiga

Swiss-managed superior quality hotel in the Taoropark. Exclusive atmosphere.
77 rooms; Tel: 38 32 51, Fax: 38 40 55; Category 2

SPORT & LEISURE

Fishing
The best spot for fishing is off the breakwater by the old fishing port and at the end of the Playa Martiánez.

Swimming
Lago de Martiánez
Architecturally impressive seawater swimming pool, consisting of several pools linked together with waterways. A large sun terrace surrounded by vegetation. Plenty of restaurants and bars offer a change of scenery.

Playa Jardín
★ Puerto de la Cruz's new 'garden beach' in the Punta Brava district below Loro Parque. Extensive sandy beach with huge gardens, terraced café, restaurant and other amenities.

Playa Martiánez
Situated quite close to the town centre. Newly renovated. A wave-machine that operates below the surface simulates sea currents.

Health and fitness
La Chiripa, spa, sauna and sport studio.
Urb. San Fernando; Casablanca-Gym, Urb. El Tope; Bahamas Gym, Avda. General Franco

Covered wagon rides
Cañadas-Trek: a covered, horse-drawn wagon ride through Tenerife's forests.
3750 ptas including meals; Tel: 908/10 99 71

Squash
Club inside the Edificio Belitope.
La Paz

Diving
Atlantic diving school based at the Hotel Maritim.
Tel: 34 45 01

Tennis
Most hotels have good tennis courts, some floodlit. There is also the *Tenniscenter Miramar (Urb. Valparaiso, Los Realejos)*

Walking
Walkers can either simply follow the marked paths or use one of the guidebooks for walking tours (these are available in good bookshops).
For guided walks, contact Gregorio in the Hotel Tigaiga, Tel: 38 32 51 or TIMAH-mountain walks, Tel: 71 02 42

ENTERTAINMENT

Andromeda/Isla de Lago nightclub
Exclusive night-club in the Lago de Martiánez area, below sea level. Features a stainless-steel dance floor beneath a dome that can be opened to expose the starlit night. International dance performances and folklore evenings are also staged here.
Daily 21.30-03.00 hrs; Avda. Colón; entrance 3650 ptas, with evening meal 6000 ptas

Bar Berlin
Bar-cafeteria serving snacks. Where the 'in-crowd' meets.
Daily 09.00 hrs until late; Avda. Venezuela, opposite the Café de Paris

Caballo Blanco
❀ A local four-piece band plays good dance music. Rustic-style restaurant. Two comfortable bars

away from the dance floor. Reasonable prices.

Daily 21.00-03.00 hrs; Promenade San Telmo, Hotel San Telmo foyer

Café de Paris

Terraced café and bistro with an international atmosphere. By the promenade. A place to see and be seen.

Daily from 10.00 hrs until late; Avda. Colón

Casino Taoro

Roulette and blackjack in the Taoro park.

Daily from 21.00 hrs; Ctra. Taoro; Entrance 500 ptas, passport required

Ex-Bar

Small, comfortable bar. Drinks and snacks.

Daily from 18.00 hrs; Avda. Venezuela, underneath Bar Berlin

Rincón del Puerto

Canarian patio with various restaurants; tapas, country wine, fish specialities. Live music from 20.00 hrs.

Daily from 10.00 hrs, by the Plaza del Charco (in the old town)

Bar Tejas Verde

Canarian musicians play atmospheric music and songs for singing along. An authentic venue where you can experience native conviviality at close quarters.

Daily 21.00-01.00 hrs; C/. Puerto Viejo 28

Discoteca Victoria

In the Hotel Tenerife Playa opposite the seawater pool. Smart atmosphere attracts a middle-aged clientele.

Daily until 04.00 hrs

INFORMATION

Oficina de Turismo

On the church square, C/. Quintana; Tel: 38 08 70, 37 02 43

SURROUNDING AREA

Aguamansa　　　　　　(D3)

★ Located on the right-hand side of the road just before it disappears into the pine forest is a trout farm that is open to the public. There is also a forestry office here that gives information about the wildlife and the local habitat. There are footpaths leading to La Caldera, a small crater and popular picnic spot where barbecue grills have been installed.

Buenavista del Norte　　(A4)

This attractive isolated village (pop. 5000) nestles in the midst of banana plantations at the end of the Isla Baja, directly beneath the steeply rising Teno hills. Locals meet to chat in the pavilion or play games on the square under the shade of the bay trees. Streets are lined with traditional houses and the 18th-century altar figures and ornate Mudéjar-style ceiling of Nuestra Señora de los Remedios church are well worth a visit.

Behind the square there is a road that leads down to a pebble beach where fishing boats are moored. About a kilometre further west is the ᴝ Mirador de Don Pompejo. This viewing platform opens up behind a rock gateway. On a clear day it is possible to make out the neighbouring island of La Palma and see the north coast as far away as Puerto de la Cruz.

Los Claveles, a simple village restaurant, has a good reputation, as it serves local specialities and an excellent country wine.
Daily 11.00-22.00 hrs; C/. Los Molinos 22; Category 3

Garachico (B3)

⚓ Garachico (pop. 5900) is a traditional Canarian village about 25 km from Puerto de la Cruz. Set in a picturesque spot on a lava peninsula, it exudes the atmosphere of a tranquil resort. Just offshore is the striking Roque de Garachico, symbol of the village. Formed from lava scree, the coast is flat and features a pretty promenade that follows the shoreline. At the western end, between the rocks, is a seawater pool.

A monument to a lifeguard, who was drowned in the spring of 1987 when an ocean earthquake sent tidal waves crashing in, stands near the Castillo San Miguel. This 16th-century fortress, which bears the coat-of-arms of the counts of Gomera and Adeje on its sturdy portal, is one of the few buildings to have survived the eruption of 1706. Founded after the Spanish conquest, Garanchico rapidly turned into a thriving centre, thanks to its harbour, from where Tenerife's wine was exported. This prosperity was brought to a brutal end, however, when the Bermeka volcano erupted. It spewed lava for 40 days, burying the opulent mansions of this flourishing port. A large part of the town and its harbour was completely destroyed. Only the tower of the Santa Ana church survived unscathed. Inside the 18th-century church that now stands in its place, the Baroque altar and statues of St Anna and St Joaquim by Luján Pérez are worth a closer look.

On the *plaza* stands a memorial in honour of Simón Bolívar, who is feted as the 'liberator of South America'. Directly behind the square lies the 17th-century palace of the counts of Gomera and Adeje, descendants of Cristóbal de Ponte, who founded the harbour around 1500. Another building that escaped the volcano's destruction is the former Franciscan monastery (Convento de San Francisco), now the Casa de Cultura. It is open to the public for cultural events, and visitors can take advantage of the opportunity to admire the fine interior and splendid cloisters.

Two restaurants here deserve mention: the *Isla Baja* is noted for its fresh fish and seafood dishes *(C/. Esteban de Ponte 5; Category 3)* and the *Miro* is a basic restaurant serving traditional fare *(Daily 10.00-22.00 hrs; C/. Conde del Palmar 12; Category 3)*. Information is available from the Ayuntamiento (town hall). *(Daily 09.00-13.00 hrs; Plaza de la Libertad 1; Tel: 83 00 00, Fax: 83 13 01)*.

La Guancha (C3)

There is a road with a fine panoramic view that goes from Realejo Alto up the steep Tigaiga incline to the rural village of Icod El Alto. Carry on through the scented pine forests until you reach La Guancha (pop. 5000). This town at the foot of the 896-m Topete was renowned for its pottery and the skills of its craftsmen. Their know-how is being passed on at the handicrafts school that has been set up here. The main thoroughfare is lined with neat, modern houses decorated with flowers. Agriculture remains the main source of income for the inhabitants. The community recently opened a *casino,* where the local youth meet every Sunday afternoon to dance. Exhibitions of local crafts are held here in the summer. A number of water galleries run along the slopes above the village.

Icod de los Viños (B3)

About 25 km west of Puerto de la Cruz lies the town of Icod de los Vinos. Founded in 1501, it now has a population of about 18 000. As the name suggests, wines are produced from the nearby vineyards, and they have earned a good reputation. The old town developed around the tiny church, but today the town centre is dominated by the modern residential blocks built up around the eastern side.

Icod is an important landmark on the tourist route because of its ancient ★ dragon tree. It is 16 m high, 6 m wide, and is widely believed to be nearly 3000 years old. It is difficult to tell exactly, as it does not have any inner rings which indicate its age; some scientists maintain that it is only a few hundred years old. This awesome specimen stands on a curve in the road to Santiago del Teide. The façade of the old building beside the tree features a carved wooden balcony, and in the inner courtyard there is a shop selling a wide array of souvenirs.

A little further along, behind the tree, lies the verdant Parque de Lorenzo Cáceres and the 16th-century church of San Marcos.

One of the treasures held within this five-nave church is a priceless silver cross from Mexico, reckoned to be one of the finest examples of silver filigree work in the world. It is on view only in the mornings. There are two pavilions nearby and various types of palm tree, jacaranda and laurels cast their shadows over this peaceful spot. A flight of steps leads from the park up to the Plaza de la Constitución, which is overlooked by some typically ornate houses.

A road winds down through banana plantations to the black, sandy beach of ✪ *Playa de San Marcos.* The sea here is ideal for swimming as the surf is not too strong. Blocks of flats and terraced cafés line the beach. In between them stands a pretty chapel decorated with stucco that can easily be overlooked. The rocky landscape is dotted with caves, some of which extend back as far as 40 m.

The *Cueva del Viento,* the deepest cave in the Canary Islands, is found in the district of El Amparo. Its full length was measured at 14 870 m. Unfortunately it is not yet open to the public, but plans have been laid to establish a research institute here and it will then be possible to explore the first 250 m.

Above La Montañeta is the ★ *Las Arenas Negras* picnic area. This is a popular spot, and barbecue grills have been set up for public use. It is also a good starting point for walks to the island's youngest volcano, Chinyero.

Places to eat in Icod: *Brisamar* which serves cakes and ice-cream on a pleasant terrace *(corner of Avda. Marítima and C/. San Marcos;*

The black sand of Playa de San Marcos near Icod de los Vinos

Category 3) and the *Caney* restaurant *(Los Moriscos; Category 3)*. *Agustín y Rosa* is a basic hotel with 14 rooms *(C/. San Sebastián 15; Tel: 81 00 85; Category 3)*. Further information is available from the Ayuntamiento *(Daily 09.00-14.00 hrs; Plaza Luis de León Huerta; Tel: 81 07 58, Fax: 81 06 69)*.

Masca (B4)

★ The tiny village of Masca lies in a wide dip between the Teno hills, and consists of just a few houses and farmsteads. An asphalt road now connects the village with the outside world and tourist buses can now reach it. A small church with a palm-shaded square lies at the heart of the village. A small museum in Lomo de Masca records the history of this remote settlement, once only accessible by bridle paths.

Mirador Garachico (B3-4)

↘↙ This viewpoint between Icod de los Vinos and Santiago del Teide looks over Garachico.

Mirador Humboldt (D3)

↘↙ This panorama named after Alexander von Humboldt is situated on the country road be-

tween La Orotava and Santa Úrsula. It was here that the German explorer and naturalist declared his enthusiasm for the Orotava valley shadowed by the volcanic Teide, and a plaque in Spanish records his words. The view is tremendous from here, but sadly the countryside is not as unspoilt as it was in Humboldt's day.

Punta de Teno (A4)

★ ☿ To reach this remote, flat coastal region and its lighthouse from Buenavista, it is necessary to pass through two road tunnels. Several tranquil bays lie hidden along the craggy coastline dotted with countless caves. When the waves roar in, the compressed air in the cavities forces the water to spurt out in giant fountains. Fishing boats moor beside the lighthouse and there is also a black sandy beach for swimmers.

Los Realejos (C3)

Los Realejos (pop. 30 000) is in fact comprised of two separate districts, Realejo Alto and Realejo Bajo, both of which lie on the steep slopes of the western Orotava valley.

Realejo Alto ('upper' Realejo)

boasts some well-preserved Canarian houses and the oldest church on Tenerife, Santiago Apóstol. The first Guanches were said to have been baptized here. The bell-tower dates from the 18th century and one of its bells was a gift from Ferdinand of Aragon, king of Spain, and his wife, queen Isabella of Castille. Inside the church the altar is adorned with a painting by an artist from the Flemish school. Directly behind the town hall, a narrow street leads to the cemetery, its entrance marked by a wonderful dragon tree.

Realejo Bajo ('lower' Realejo) is a modern town with some new residential blocks and attractive cafés. El Socorro is the only proper beach here. Throughout the year powerful waves crash on the shore, making it a popular haunt for surfers – only good swimmers should venture out into the strong currents. A number of fish restaurants with car parking facilities can also be found in the vicinity. Access to the beach is from the northern coast road in the direction of Icod de los Viños, and the exit is signposted.

The coastal region is occupied by a number of holiday developments, namely Romántica I, Romántica II, La Longuera (with shops) and El Toscal. In the La Montañeta district a hill of volcanic ash is crowned by a tiny, white chapel, and is a popular destination among the locals. On the road to La Luz stands a veritable jewel of Canarian architecture, in the form of an old monastery with a magnificent inner courtyard. Now restored with fastidious attention to detail

and at considerable cost, the building has been converted into a popular restaurant, known appropriately enough as El Monasterio. Quite apart from the food, the vaulting in the cellars, and the vast range of wines, the restaurant make this a worthwhile visit. Its menu is varied, featuring mainly meat dishes, and is very reasonably priced *(Open from 10.00 hrs; Category 2)*. *Villa Nueva* restaurant is also recommended for its elegant but friendly atmosphere. International and Canarian dishes are served *(Daily, except Wednesday; 12.00-15.00 and 18.00-23.00 hrs)*. One hotel is worth mentioning: the *Tierra de Oro* is a spa hotel. Situated in a quiet spot along the edge of town, this venue offers 80 beds, a vegetarian restaurant and a medical consultant, who will recommend a course of treatment upon request *(Tel: 34 10 00; Hotel buses; Category 2)*.

Los Silos (B4)

This pretty village (pop. 5400) lies on the Isla Baja. Nuestra Señora de la Luz, a small, 20th-century neo-classical church, stands by the plaza. Inside, the central highlight is a figure of Cristo de la Misericordia (17th century) sculpted by Juan de Mesa of Seville. To get to the coast, some 2 km away, turn off by the petrol station at the far end of the village. There are a number of modern developments here as well as a seawater pool. A narrow road winds among the banana plantations along the lava coast and leads to the minuscule fishing village of La Caleta, which has a small black sand beach.

Cliffs and chasms

*Hikers will be rewarded with some stunning views
in this rugged part of the island*

The stretch of coastline between Santa Úrsula and Tacoronte is bordered with cliffs, averaging around 200 m in height. The landscape, furrowed by deep gorges or *barrancos*, rises gently up towards the mountain ridge that forms the island's backbone, an area known as the Cumbre Dorsal. The slopes are cultivated with terraced fields and scattered with villages and hamlets. The Cumbre Dorsal reaches its highest peak at 2000 m where the giant Las Cañadas crater is, and drops down to 600 m where it levels out into the La Laguna plain. A band of clouds lingers over the flat terrain and so La Laguna is often overcast. To the north, the plain dips down to the sea via the Valle de Guerra and the Valle de Tejina, while to the south lies the broad bay (5 km wide) of Santa Cruz de Tenerife, where huge cargo vessels dock and unload. The climate in this sheltered bay is hot and humid. The jagged peaks of the grey Anaga moun-

tain range form a stunning backdrop to the Santa Cruz skyline. Rising in places to 1000 m and with their lower slopes and inaccessible valleys covered with dense laurel woods, the Anagas dominate the far north-eastern corner of the island.

BAJAMAR

(**D1**) This quiet, popular resort lies between the foothills of the Anaga mountains and the sea. Both sides of the valley are lined with houses, hotel complexes and bungalows. A promenade along the coast leads to a seawater pool. There is a small, black sandy beach nearby, but the strong surf makes it difficult to swim. For day hikers, the Anaga mountains are easily accessible from here. Their steep rock faces dominate the surrounding landscape.

HOTELS

Delfín
A centrally-located hotel complex situated by the sea, with video, discotheque and bar, tennis courts and a freshwater swim-

*Hedges of prickly pears face the
ragged cliffs of the north-east coast*

ming pool in the garden.
66 rooms; Avda. del Sol 39; Tel: 54 02 00, Fax: 54 02 00; Category 1

Océano
Well-run hotel with a magnificent garden and a health centre that has a variety of nutritional programmes. 100 of the apartments have a sea view.
Punta del Hidalgo; Tel: 54 11 12; Category 2

INFORMATION

Ayuntamiento
Daily 09.00-14.00 hrs; La Plaza; Tel: 54 11 20

LA LAGUNA

(E2) La Laguna (pop. 110 000) lies on a broad flat plain, an unusual geographical feature for the northern part of the island. Narrow streets laid out in a kind of chequer-board pattern are lined with many old houses and mansions. Some date as far back as 1497, when Alonso Fernández de Lugo founded La Laguna and made it the island's capital. A neo-classical town hall stands in the shady Plaza del Adelantado and the old chapels, churches, monasteries and cathedrals house many priceless art treasures. The only bishop in the Canary Islands has his residence here and the university, which offers a full range of courses, serves all seven islands. The modern university premises are mostly located around the town centre.

SIGHTS

Cathedral
When La Laguna became a bishopric in 1818, renovation work began immediately on the Los Remedios parish church, which

was first founded in 1515. Now transformed into a cathedral, it is particularly interesting for its marble pulpit (1767), a Baroque retable decorated with paintings by Hendrik Van Balen (Van Dyck's master), side altars with statues by Luján de Pérez, and its silverwork. Behind the high altar lies the grave of the town's founder, Alonso Fernández de Lugo.
C/. Obispo Rey Redondo

Nuestra Señora de la Concepción

★ This 16th-century church, which has undergone very few modifications over the centuries, is one of the jewels of Tenerife's national heritage. The tower was built in Mudéjar style and the wooden interior, though a little gloomy, has a splendid pulpit made of carved cedarwood and statues by Estévez.
C/. Obispo Rey Redondo

Museo de la Ciencia y del Cosmos

Since it opened in 1993, this natural science museum has been taking a look at the universe in fascinating, and often disconcerting, displays explaining the solar system, the appearance of life on earth and the relationship between mankind and the cosmos. Visitors are invited to watch a range of interesting experiments.
Daily (except Monday) 10.00–20.00 hrs; Vía Láctea; Entrance: 200 ptas

Fortuny

This restaurant serves up typical Canarian dishes.
Daily 12.00–22.00 hrs; La Esperanza; Category 2

Aguere

Basic hotel in the centre of town with 32 rooms.
C/. Obispo Rey Redondo 57; Tel: 25 94 90; Category 3

C/. Obispo Rey Redondo 1; Tel: 60 11 00, Fax: 60 11 02

LA MATANZA DE ACENTEJO

(D2) La Matanza means 'slaughter' and refers to a battle that took place on 31 May 1494, when the Spanish suffered a humiliating defeat in their first confrontation with the Guanches. Two hills are the symbol for this village (pop. 5000), which extends from the coast to a forest known as Bosque de la Esperanza. The surrounding region is renowned for its wine.

Perched on rocks, the village of El Caletón is separated from the sea by a small, black sandy beach. Further up, on the edge of the cliff, the apartment blocks of El Puntillo del Sol, a holiday village, cling to the rocks. The main village lies above the motorway. The restaurants and bars along the old road offer some fine views over the north-west coast. Chicken forms the basis of this area's speciality dishes.

Museo Cooperativo AYT-M-Maheh

Here, in the old town hall, the history of traditional Canarian sports, such as stick fighting, stone-lifting and *lucha canaria* (wrestling; see page 19) is documented.

Daily (except Monday) 09.30-13.00 and 15.30-18.00 hrs; C/. Real; Entrance: 200 ptas, 400 ptas with performance

(wrestling; see page 19)

RESTAURANTS

Casa Juan

Smoked salmon, eels and mackerel are the speciality dishes on offer in this attractively furnished, family-run concern.

Daily (except Monday) 12.00-22.00 hrs; Camino de Acentejo 29; Category 2

La Duela

◁⟩ There is a fabulous view from the roof terrace of this simple restaurant. Kid a speciality.

Daily 11.00-22.00 hrs; C/. La Toca/ San Antonio; Category 3

INFORMATION

Ayuntamiento

Ctra. General; Tel: 57 71 97, Fax: 57 78 71

PUNTA DEL HIDALGO

(D-E1) This peaceful holiday resort is still, at heart, a typical fishing village. To enable tourists to reach this rather inaccessible spot, a coastal road was dug out of the Anaga rock. The hotels on the flat peninsula next to the rocky coastline have seawater swimming pools and the reefs are ideal for sea-fishing. About a kilometre beyond the village the road ends with a roundabout. This vantage point offers a fine view out over the eastern edge of the Anaga mountains and the rocky offshore island of Los Hermanos. Punta del Hidalgo makes a good starting-point for walking tours of the Anagas.

RESTAURANTS

La Isla

Fresh fish a speciality. Folk evenings on Tuesday and Friday.

Daily 11.00-23.00 hrs; Avda. Marítima; Category 2

Cafe Melita

◁⟩ Well-run café with fine panoramic view. Large selection of cakes and pastries.

Daily from 10.00 hrs; Ctra. La Punta

INFORMATION

Ayuntamiento

Daily 09.00-14.00 hrs; La Plaza; Tel: 54 11 20

SAN ANDRÉS

(E-F1) With its squares and steep mountain slopes studded with pretty, white houses, this picturesque fishing village, located 8 km from Santa Cruz, is rather reminiscent of an Indian pueblo and certainly merits a visit. It is especially reputed for its simple, satisfying seafood restaurants along the water's edge. On the village outskirts lie the ruins of a watchtower that was built to forewarn islanders of imminent pirate attacks. A little further on, Saharan sand gleams in the sun. The yellow sand for this beach was transported here from Africa in the 1970s in order to fulfil the expectations of the increasing numbers of holidaymakers descending on the island. It is known as the ★ *Playa de las Teresitas*. Shade is supplied by clusters of evergreen palms and an embankment protects bathers from rough seas. The beach, which is about 2 km long, is dominated to the west by the rocky slopes of the Anaga mountains. The coastal road to the north-east winds its way up to the impressive panorama at ◁▷ Punta de los Órganos. The eastern coastline all the way down to Candelaria is visible from this point. The black sand beaches of Playa de Burro and the nudist Playa las Gaviotas are situated to the east.

RESTAURANT

La Langostera
Fish and seafood in a pleasant, relaxed atmosphere.
Daily (except Monday) 12.00-23.00 hrs; Avda. El Dique 14

INFORMATION

Oficina de Turismo
Daily 09.00-13.00 and 16.00-19.00 hrs; Cabildo, Plaza de España; Tel: 60 55 00, Fax: 60 57 81

SANTA CRUZ DE TENERIFE

(E2) The more attractive side of this city and port (pop. 200 000) is not evident at first sight, but once you begin exploring it you will soon discover that there are as many historic squares and buildings, parks and boulevards as there are futuristic multi-storey blocks that accommodate the many banks and offices. Santa Cruz, the capital of the region and the island, is a port, a trading centre and a distribution centre. It is situated in a sheltered bay at the foot of the Anaga massif and owes its importance to the development of the port. Thanks to its geographical position at the crossroads of the main Atlantic trading routes, it has been one of Spain's principal ports since the mid-17th century.

The history of Santa Cruz goes back over 500 years to 3 May 1492 when the Spanish conquistadors landed on what was then

Tons of yellow sand from the Sahara Desert were shipped over to embellish Playa de las Teresitas

called Añaza beach. They built their first fortress here and set about conquering the rest of the island. When the harbour at Garachico was destroyed, the one at Santa Cruz became the main distribution point for the island. But it was exposed and vulnerable to attack by pirates, so new fortifications were necessary and a military governor was appointed to take responsibility for defence. On 25 July 1797, one year after the port had received sole authorization to trade with America, Admiral Nelson attacked. His objective was to board two galleons laden with silver from Mexico. During the ensuing battle, Nelson lost his right arm. In 1822 Santa Cruz officially became the capital of the Canary Islands.

SIGHTS

Harbour

Ships from all over Europe, central and southern America, Africa and Asia use the port. Tankers unload their oil cargoes at the refinery to the west of the town. Several jetfoils and ferries leave for Gran Canaria every day.

Nuestra Señora de la Concepción

With a foundation stone that was laid by the Spanish conquistadors in 1502, this church is the oldest in Santa Cruz, but in 1652 it fell victim to fire and was not fully restored until the 18th century. The interior of the five-naved church was completed in ornate Baroque style. Of particular interest are the 'Dolorosa' figures by Luján Pérez, the jasper 'Concepción' by Estévez at the high altar and the carved choir stalls.

The cross that the Spanish conquerors planted on the beach and a Gothic statue of the Virgin Mary are kept here, together with the flags that Admiral Nelson left behind. Unfortunately, the church is presently closed for restoration work.
C/. Domínguez Alfonso, by the Barranco de Santos

Parque Municipal Garcia Sanabria

Completed in 1930, this park was named after the popular mayor who designed its layout. Alongside native trees and bushes stand statues of some of the town's eminent citizens and famous artists.
C/. Méndez Núñez

Plaza de la Candelaria

This lovely rectangular square bordered with benches and shops is a pedestrian area. The Carrara marble statue that stands in the centre was made in 1778 by the Italian sculptor Antonio Canova and depicts the patron saint of the Canary Islands looking down on four Guanche chieftains.

Plaza de España

On this busy square that looks out to sea the cruciform Monumento de los Caídos commemorates the dead of the Spanish Civil War. A fine view of the city and harbour awaits visitors who take the lift to the top.

Plaza de Weyler

A beautiful marble fountain forms the centrepiece of this square. Star-shaped paths interspersed with flower beds all converge towards it, and in the background stands the neo-classical Capitanía General building, which was erected by General

Valeriano Weyler at the end of the 19th century.

MUSEUMS

Museo Arqueológico

Items unearthed in the caves where the Guanches lived, such as tools, cutlery, weapons and mummies, are exhibited here.
Daily 09.00-13.00 and 16.00-18.00 hrs; Plaza de España; Entrance: 200 ptas

Museo Municipal de Bellas Artes

Attractions in this fine art museum include displays of weapons and coin collections, as well as an extensive art gallery featuring paintings by Brueghel, Ribera and Jordaens (among others) and sculptures by Luján and Capuz. There is a library on the upper floor.
Daily 13.00-19.00 hrs; C/. José Murphy 4; Entrance free

RESTAURANTS

El Líbano

Lebanese and international cuisine. Busy at lunchtime.
Daily 12.00-16.00 and 20.00-24.00 hrs; C/. Santiago Cuadrado 36; Category 2

Olympo

Fast food or a full set menu. Terrace with view of the harbour and Plaza de España.
Daily 10.00-24.00 hrs. Plaza de España/Casa de los Balcones; Category 2

Café del Príncipe

Good selection of cakes; snacks are served in the garden café.
Daily 09.00-24.00 hrs; Plaza del Príncipe; Category 2

SHOPPING

Calle del Castillo

This pedestrianized zone is the best shopping street on Tenerife.

Flea market

★ ❖ A flea market is held every Sunday morning between 09.00 and 14.00 hrs around the Mercado de Nuestra Señora de África. Cheap junk to quality goods on sale.

Mercado de Nuestra Señora de África

❖ This oriental-style building houses the fresh fruit, vegetable and meat market. It's the place to see the authentic Tenerife. In a nearby lane lined with covered stalls, traders sell everything from cheap souvenirs to chamber pots. Expect to haggle.
C/. San Sebastián

HOTELS

Santa Cruz is not a tourist resort, so the hotels here are intended primarily for business people.

Atlántico

New hotel in the city centre, but situated in the pedestrian zone away from all the traffic noise.
60 rooms; C/. del Castillo; Tel: 24 63 75, Fax: 24 63 78; Category 2

Mencey

The city's top hotel. Stylishly furnished with a swimming pool and set in a delightful garden. This is where King Juan Carlos and Queen Sofía often stay when visiting Tenerife.
286 rooms; C/. Dr José Neveiras 38; Tel: 27 67 00, Fax: 28 00 17; Category 1

A Bordo

Café-restaurant with plenty of atmosphere.
Avda. Anaga

Discoteca KU

This is the best disco in Santa Cruz. Up-to-date with an international feel.
Parque la Granja

Olé

Bar/pub.
Rambla General Franco

Tasca Tosca

Friendly meeting place favoured by the Santa Cruz elite and local celebrities.
Avda. Anaga

Vips

Bar/pub.
Rambla General Franco

INFORMATION

Oficina di Turismo

Daily 09.00-13.00 and 16.00-19.00 hrs; Cabildo, Plaza de España; Tel: 60 55 00, Fax: 60 57 81

SURROUNDING AREA

Anaga mountains   **(E-F1)**
★ ☙ The Anaga massif covers practically the whole of the north-eastern corner of Tenerife. This craggy and jagged mountain range is furrowed with deep valleys and gorges. On all three coasts, the mountain sides drop precipitously down to the sea. The highest point, the Taborno, reaches a height of 1020 m above sea level. Although beautiful, it is one of the wildest and most deserted regions on the island. The lower slopes, densely overgrown with laurel trees, form the Bosque de las Mercedes. Tree heath and broom take over at about 800 m, while moss and lichen coat the bare basalt rocks that tower up to the sky.

There is a picturesque drive north that's worth taking. It leaves from La Laguna and passes through the mountain village of Las Mercedes. The first viewpoint you come to is the Mirador de Jardina, situated by a bend in the road above Las Mercedes. Set in a forest clearing a few kilometres further on stands the Cruz del Carmen guesthouse and pilgrims' chapel. After about another kilometre, the road branches off to the right, in the direction of the Pico del Inglés. From the top of this peak, the view extends across the Anagas to Teide and, on a clear day, you can see the neighbouring island of Gran Canaria. The road carries on uphill along the ridge with views over the coastlines on either side. At the junction, carry straight on to the El Bailadero restaurant. From here the road leads down to Chamorga, but it does not go all the way to the coast. You can take a detour to the north-eastern tip of the island on foot, where you will glimpse an abandoned lighthouse and a small sandy beach.

Instead of continuing on to Chamorga, turn left at the last road junction and follow the road through a tunnel and down to Taganana where the hillsides are dotted with white houses. Stop off for a glass of the excellent country wine in one of the bodegas. A few kilometres beyond the cobbled streets of Taganana is Los Roques beach, where the fish restaurants that cling to the rocks do a good trade with the tourists. The village of Almáciga sits on a small sandy beach about a kilometre further on. Return through the tunnel and head south across the peninsula through wild terrain and down to San Andrés on the opposite coast.

Cumbre Dorsal (D-E 2-3)

★ ◁◁ The road that follows the narrow Cumbre Dorsal mountain range divides the island into two. It offers some fine views as it rises from 600 m to 2300 m above sea level, where the giant Cañadas crater begins. Come off the motorway near La Laguna and follow signs to La Esperanza. The sides of the road are lined with yellow and white broom until you reach La Esperanza, a village where sheep and pigs are bred. From this point on, the road is shaded by eucalyptus trees and Canarian pines that release a refreshing scent. About 4 km further on a small restaurant and picnic site known as Las Raíces comes into view. Take a break near Montaña Grande to enjoy a bird's eye view of Santa Cruz de Tenerife, La Laguna and the northern airport way below. Further on, Mirador Ortuño provides a marvellous opportunity to survey the northern half of the island. Turn right toward Mirador de Las Cumbres a short distance on and, after about 200 m, the southern half of the island becomes visible. On a clear day, Gran Canaria may appear out of the clouds. After a further 700 m, the north coast emerges, at which point you may be able to pick out the western island of La Palma through the haze. At this altitude the vegetation becomes sparser and dense pine forests flank either side of the road. The road meanders through a gorge and gives you a chance to study the colourful volcanic rock formations. The TV transmitters and Izaña meteorological observatory point skyward like a line of white rockets. El Portillo and the Cañadas crater now lie just ahead.

Radazul (E2)

This little town straddles the motorway and has developed into a popular resort in recent years. The residential blocks, apartments and expensive villas are owned for the most part by wealthy foreigners and a handful of rich islanders. Luxury yachts are moored in the *Club de Mar Radazul* marina which is sheltered by a 100 m cliff and can accommodate about 100 boats. Most of the berths here are occupied by local boats for long-term storage and consequently very few outsiders can stop over. Entering the port does not involve any difficult manoeuvres, and Radazul can even be entered at night, because the breakwater stands out clearly against the cliffs and the tall apartment blocks.

Tabaiba (E2)

About 8 km to the south of Santa Cruz, the motorway passes through Tabaiba. There is a smallish industrial estate situated at the water's edge, while to the north a number of locally-owned holiday villas have been built.

SANTA ÚRSULA

(D3) This rather modest village (pop. 8500) has a church with some fine ceiling paintings and a lovely little palm-shaded square. Handicraft workshops and bars line the main thoroughfare and an old wine press stands by the La Quinta motorway exit. To reach the Vista Paraíso viewpoint which is situated on rocks 260 m above the town, take the La Orotava motorway exit. The bridge over the motorway leads to the villa quarter.

RESTAURANTS

Los Corales
◁▷ Good fish and seafood restaurant. Panoramic view.
Daily 12.00-22.00 hrs; Cuesta de la Villa 60; Category 2

Vista Paraíso
◁▷ Café with panoramic terrace, perilously positioned at the top of the cliff. Renowned for its home-made cakes and tarts. Also good for savoury snacks.
Daily (except Sunday) 10.00-19.00 hrs

INFORMATION

Ayuntamiento
Plaza General Franco 13, Tel: 30 00 25, Fax: 30 16 40

SAUZAL

(D2) The most attractive route to this village (pop. 6200) on the edge of the 300-m high crag is via the Valle de los Ángeles. Leave the motorway at La Matanza de Acentejo and turn downhill to the right, past El Puntillo del Sol and Los Naranjeros. The steep, narrow coast road down to the harbour at Sauzal, Puertito de Sauzal, is not for the faint-hearted. The village is noted for its Moorish-style domed church. Near the motorway turn-off, a 16th-century mansion built beneath a huge boulder houses the ★ Casa del Vino wine museum *(Daily 11.00-20.00 hrs; Entrance free)*. Attractions here include a tasting room, a restaurant and a terraced café with a breathtaking view of the ◁▷ north coast.

RESTAURANT

San Nicolás
Fish restaurant with a wide selection of fresh catch.
Daily (except Tuesday) 12.00-24.00 hrs; Ctra. General de Sauzal; Category 3

INFORMATION

Ayuntamiento
C/. de la Constitución 3; Tel: 57 00 00, Fax: 57 09 73

TACORONTE

(D2) This busy market town (pop. 17 000) is situated in one of the island's most fertile regions. The wine, potatoes and other vegetables produced here are sold in the *mercado* at very reasonable prices. The market is on the right-hand side of the road to Valle de Guerra and is open on Saturday from 12.00 to 17.00 hrs and Sunday from 10.00 to 14.00 hrs. The same road leads to the town centre, where the 17th-century church of San Agustín harbours one of the island's most venerated statues of Christ (Cristo de los Dolores). Diagonally opposite the church stands a fine specimen of a dragon tree. Hidden away in the lower town is the church of Santa Catalina with its Mudéjar-style tower (16th-18th century), which features a beautifully-carved ceiling panel, Luján Pérez's *Inmaculada*, a picture of the *Ánimas* by Quintana, and a high altar richly ornamented with Mexican silverwork. The square outside is lined with Indian laurels. About 2 km along the road to Valle de Guerra, there is a left-hand turn that takes you down a winding road to Mesa del Mar and El Prix.

RESTAURANT

El Campo
Typical Canarian restaurant with menu to match.
Daily (except Monday) 12.00-15.00 and 18.00-23.00 hrs; Ctra. General 35, Los Naranjeros; Category 3

INFORMATION

Policía Municipal
Plaza del Cristo; Tel: 56 13 50, Fax: 56 25 90

VALLE DE GUERRA

(**D2**) The fertile valley and the village itself were named after a war hero, whose loyal services were rewarded with this land by Alonso Fernández de Lugo after the island's conquest. Bananas and strelitzia grow abundantly in this region. Just outside the village, the early 18th-century residence that once belonged to the aristocratic Guerra family overlooks the valley. The house has been transformed into a local history museum, the *Museo Casa de la Carta*.

MUSEUM

Museo Etnográfico
Interesting museum where you can discover how the islanders lived during the colonial era.
Daily (except Friday) 10.00-13.00 and 16.00-18.00 hrs; Entrance: 200 ptas

INFORMATION

Ayuntamiento
La Laguna, C/. Obispo Rey Redondo 1; Tel: 26 10 11

LA VICTORIA DE ACENTEJO

(**D2**) This unassuming village (pop. 7100), is home to craftsmen, farmers and wine-growers. It is best known for its church, which features a beautiful ornate silver altar from Mexico and a Mudéjar-style carved wooden ceiling.

RESTAURANT

Mesón de Paco
They really know how to prepare fish and seafood here.
Daily (except Monday) 12.00-16.00 and 18.00-22.00 hrs; Ctra. General del Norte 135; Category 2

INFORMATION

Ayuntamiento
Plaza Rodríguez Lara; Tel: 58 00 31, Fax: 58 01 76

A lunar landscape

This spectacular volcanic backdrop took shape
more than a quarter of a million years ago

The road between La Orotava and Aguamansa passes through dense forest and winds down towards El Portillo de las Cañadas, the doorway to the ★ *Parque Nacional de las Cañadas del Teide* in the heart of Tenerife (**C4**). This immense national park was declared a protected site in 1954. With its bizarre lunar landscape and rock formations, it is one of the most interesting places to visit on the island.

You won't have gone very far into the park with its covering of pumice stone before the stone desert of the Caldera de las Cañadas appears underneath a deep blue sky. This volcanic depression formed by the collapse of the volcano's cone, referred to by geologists as a caldera, lies at about 2000 m above sea level. On the northern side of the crater stands the 3718-m high Pico del Teide, while to the south it is flanked by steep cliffs that rise to a height of 500 m. With a circumference of 45 km and a

The Pico del Teide, the 'Roof of Tenerife', dominates the landscape

diameter of 17 km, this vast nature reserve covers a total surface area of 13 571 hectares and is the largest in Spain.

It's worth paying a visit to the Visitor Centre (*Centro de visitantes*) before exploring the area, where displays and English-language recordings provide some insight into the geological, biological and historical background of the region.

Scientists believe that the caldera was probably formed around 300 000 years ago. A 3000-m high volcanic mountain once stood where the crater is now. Many scientists believe that this was once the site of a shield volcano. Typically, a shield volcano has a relatively thin layer of outer rock, which will give way to pressure from the liquid rock bubbling away beneath it. The volcanic cone at the site of the present caldera would therefore have collapsed as gases caused the magma reservoir to erupt.

Across the Cañadas (Spanish for ravines) de la Caldera, a variety of different rock formations and expanses of multi-coloured scoria occur. Layers of cooled lava, oxidized into various hues, extend for kilometres across the sandy Llano de Ucanca (Ucanca plain). At the edge of the plain, metre-high lumps of basalt and chunks of gleaming black obsidian lie as though they have been hurled across the landscape at random. The rock formations known as Los Roques (opposite the state-run hotel), the Parador Nacional, and the shimmering blue-green Los Azulejos and Zapato de la Reina (Queen's Shoe) formations further south, are particularly impressive. Beyond the cliffs rise Cerrillar, Chiqueros, Colmenas and Guajara (2717 m above sea level), the highest peaks in the Cañadas.

The scenery here has often been compared to a lunar landscape and from a distance it is certainly a valid comparison, but a closer inspection reveals vegetation emerging from between the lava and rock. Given the altitude and the type of terrain, it is astonishing that there are 45 species of plant that thrive in this environment, and several of these are endemic. The most common shrub that flourishes on the stretches of pumice stone and volcanic scoria is *codéso* or laburnum. This spiky shrub with twigs like bottle brushes is green in winter, but in spring the whole landscape is brightened with its yellow blossoms. Other typical Teide plants are the pinkish-white Teide broom and the *tajinaste rojo,* the 'Pride of Tenerife'. This plant can often be seen growing in clusters on the slopes of the caldera; it can reach a height of 2 m, making it the tallest plant in the park. One botanical rarity is the Teide violet. It survives on the dry pumice at a height of 3200 m above sea level, where it remains carefully camouflaged between the rocks and rarely shows its face. It is just one of the many plant species that thrive nowhere else but in the clean, crystal-clear air of the Teide National Park.

Compared to the flora, the fauna is much less varied. Wild cats, mountain rabbits, and hedgehogs are the only vertebrates that can survive at these heights, although there are a number of bird species. Sparrow hawks and kestrels are fairly common, and robins and swallows abound. The unusual blue-feathered Teide finch is endemic to the island.

MARCO POLO SELECTION: THE NATIONAL PARK

1 Road to the Cañadas crater
This road winds its way up 2000 m and passes through dense pine forests before reaching the bizarre Cañadas landscape. Magnificent views

over the whole island
(page 63)

2 Cable car to the top of Pico del Teide
The least strenuous way to reach the highest point on Tenerife (page 65)

The easiest way to reach the summit of the volcano is via cable car. It takes about 10 minutes to make the ascent of ★ ◁▷ *Pico del Teide*. The lift departs from the centre of the park, at about 2300 m above sea level. *Ascents: Daily 09.00-18.00 hrs, every 30 minutes; Descents: Daily 09.00-18.45 hrs.* The cable car service does not operate when strong winds are blowing; the road to the crater is not open to the public.

The state-run hotel, the Parador Nacional Las Cañadas del Teide *(23 rooms; Tel: 38 64 15; Category 1)* will be closed shortly for renovation.

Climbing Teide on foot

Serious hikers and mountaineers can climb Mount Teide on foot. The best time to make this excursion is between May and October. You don't need to be a hardened climber to make the trip, but bear in mind that it is a four hour climb. The prerequisites are a sound constitution, windproof clothing and sturdy shoes. Beyond El Portillo de la Caldera, about 40 km along the main Cañadas road, there is a track that branches off towards the Montaña Blanca. At this juncture stands a detailed, large-scale map that indicates the route to the summit.

The climb starts with a steep, gravel track that ascends through lava scree and pumice stone terrain. After about an hour's hike, there is a point at which the path becomes a little more difficult to negotiate as the ground is covered in slippery scoria. Once you reach the level of the Montaña Blanca, there is a steep track that veers off to the left. This is a short-cut but the going is a little harder. Otherwise, keep to the main footpath, which winds its way gently up in broad curves. After about two more hours, you will come to another footpath that forks off to the left, leading you to the Alta Vista mountain hut (3260 m). In the summer months, this hut is normally open from 17.00 to 10.00 hrs, but in the winter it remains closed. If you wish to spend the night in this refuge, it is best to reserve a bed in advance. You can do this through the ICONA office in Aguamansa (*Tel: 33 07 01*) – the organization that administers and polices the park protection.

Before embarking on the last leg to the summit and the cable-car station, it is worthwhile taking a short detour to the *Cueva del Hielo* (Ice Cave). Take the path that branches off to the right and, after a 15-minute walk, you will come to the cave entrance. Make sure to take an extra layer of clothing with you if you plan on making this detour. The temperature inside the cave is so low that the pool of water there is always frozen. Icicles hang from the ceiling all the year round and the snowdrifts never seem to melt.

Back on the main path, a 20 minute walk brings you to the ICONA path leading to the cable-car station. The final steep ascent to the edge of the crater takes a further 20 minutes. Sulphurous steam rises from fissures in the rock and if you've got numb fingers they will be quickly thawed if held over the warm vapour. Watching the sun set from the top of Mount Teide is an unforgettable experience.

Rugged beauty

*The rural, unspoilt side of Tenerife lies
to the east of Teide*

This stretch of coastline, which goes from Santa Cruz to Los Cristianos, is the area least frequented by tourists. If you follow the motorway along the east coast, all you will see is sand, stone and shingle. The monotony of the arid landscape is occasionally broken by glimpses of the green wooded slopes of the Cumbre Dorsal. If, on the other hand, you follow the old country road, the *carretera,* further inland, you will pass through a fertile region of meadows and cultivated land. The Güímar valley, the counterpart to the Orotava valley, is particularly picturesque and the conditions here are ideal for the cultivation of a wide variety of fruit and vegetables. The road runs through modest, unspoilt villages whose inhabitants see little of tourism. The majority of people who live in these parts earn their living from farming, fishing and cottage industries. In the bigger towns such

as Arafo and Güímar, there are a number of attractive chalets and holiday homes, but the majority of these are owned by Spaniards from the mainland who come over to Tenerife for the duration of the summer.

This region in the south-east of the island remains relatively unaffected by tourism. There are, nevertheless, numerous places of interest: beach resorts, historic Guanche sites, white-washed villages and lunar landscapes.

GÜÍMAR

(**D3**) Separated from the Orotava valley by the Cumbre Dorsal, the Güímar valley lies on the eastern side of the mountain ridge. Not quite so fertile as the Orotava valley, which traps the clouds and their moisture, the Güímar valley has nevertheless been successfully cultivated by its inhabitants who grow a wide variety of fruit and vegetables, including bananas, tomatoes and potatoes.

Twenty-five kilometres southwest of Santa Cruz, the small town of Güímar (pop. 14 500) nestles in the heart of the valley.

View over Vilaflor, Tenerife's highest village, surrounded by sparse pine forest

The 18th-century church of San Pedro, which stands beside the main square, features a picture of St Peter by de la Oliva and an impressive ornate pulpit. The burial sites and remains of dwellings found in this region indicate that in pre-Hispanic times Güímar was inhabited by the Guanches. At the time of the Spanish Conquest, it was ruled by the Mencey Añataerve who was converted to Christianity and ended up fighting for the Spanish Crown. For a great view of the town and valley, go up to the ★ ◥◤ *Mirador de Don Martín*. From here you can see as far as Santa Cruz and the Anaga mountains. Four kilometres west of the town lies the port of Puerto de Güímar which has a small white sandy beach. There is a typical restaurant here called the *Casa Eloy (Category 3)* that offers a wide selection of fish and meat dishes. A good road wends its way up from Güímar through Arafo to the Cumbre Dorsal and then joins the main Cañadas road.

INFORMATION

Policía Municipal
Tel: 51 01 14

SURROUNDING AREA

Arafo (D3)
The majority of the houses in this village (pop. 4100) are not just bare brick, as they are in most other villages, but have been neatly rendered. On the outskirts stands an old Canarian pine, known as the 'Lord's Pine'. In the village church of San Juan Degollado there is a statue by Luján Pérez. A steep but well-tended asphalt road ascends past small farmsteads up to the Cumbre Dorsal and the pine forest. ◥◤ This road affords some fine views over the Güímar valley and the Atlantic. On a clear day, the island of Gran Canaria is visible.

Arico (D4-5)
The district of Arico (pop. 4600) is composed of three towns – Arico Viejo, Arico El Nuevo and Lomo de Arico – as well as a few smaller settlements scattered across the hillsides. Poris de Abona is a small fishing village to the north of Punta de Abona and the lighthouse. The Moorish-style church of San Juan Bautista (17th century) in Arico El Nuevo shows a clear Portuguese influence, and

View over the Nuestra Señora de la Candelaria pilgrims church

many of the whitewashed houses still have very old doors and shutters painted in vivid green. For a taste of the regional cooking, try the *Chinchorro restaurant (Category 3)* in Poris de Abona.

Candelaria (E3)

★ ✪ The white tower of the basilica in Candelaria is visible from afar. Located on the edge of a vast square right next to the beach, this church is dedicated to the Candlemas Madonna, Candelaria, who is worshipped as the protectress of the Canary Islands. The statue most venerated by the Canary islanders is here. According to legend, years before Christianity swept the island, two Guanche goatherds found the statue of Mary washed up on the beach of Chimisay, now El

Socorro. Where this dark-hued Madonna came from is not clear. Some say that it was from a boat that had foundered during a storm. The legend also has it that when one of the herdsman threw a stone at the statue in an attempt to smash it, his arm immediately became paralysed. The two men decided to take the statue to their king, the Mencey of Güímar, who placed it in a cave. Followers of Diego de Herrera, the ruler of Lanzarote, then stole the statue and installed it in a monastery on Lanzarote, and soon strange things started to happen. When the servers entered the chapel in the morning, they regularly found the statue with its face toward the wall. Every day they turned it back round, but the next morning it was again found with its face back to the wall. The locals were alarmed by these mysterious happenings, which they linked to the theft of the statue, and so it was decided that it should be returned to Tenerife. Thus began the pilgrimages to see the miraculous Madonna. Every year thousands of Canary islanders flock to Candelaria on 14 and 15 August to pay homage to the Virgin Mary. The huge square in front of the church provides the perfect stage for the proceedings. On the seaward side of the square 10 statues of Guanche kings stand guard.

Candelaria (pop. 10 600) has an attractive old town with white-washed houses featuring the traditional wooden balcony. Colourful boats in the harbour complete this picturesque scene, complemented by a clean, lava beach below the square. New residences and holiday complexes have been built around the town.

Recommended restaurants: *Casa José (Avda. Generalísimo 3; Category 3)* and the *Playa Mar (C/. Obispo Pérez Cáceres; Category 3)*. Recommended hotels: *Tenerife Tour (98 rooms; Avda. Generalísimo 170; Tel: 50 02 00, Fax: 50 23 63; Category 3)* and *Punta del Rey (437 rooms; Tel: 50 18 99, Fax: 50 00 91; Category 2)*. For tourist information, contact the Ayuntamiento *(Tel: 50 08 00, Fax: 50 08 08)*.

Fasnia (D4)

On the road that links Güímar to Fasnia, you will cross a barren, rocky region where nothing but cacti and coarse weeds grow. At every turn, this winding road offers breathtaking views of the precipitous deep *barrancos* in between the many caves that have been carved out of the great walls of soft tufa rock that you will see on either side of the road.

The impoverished village of Fasnia (pop. 2500) nestles above a mountain of volcanic ash (202 m) on which the Nuestra Señora de los Dolores was built. In 1705 the village was almost destroyed by lava spewing from the Volcán de Fasnia (2220 m). Luckily, the lava flow came to a stop just before reaching the village. Beneath the settlement is a small sheltered bay with black lava sand.

Granadilla de Abona (D5)

This little town 10 km north of Reina Sofía airport is an important crossroads in the island's road network where the main north-south and east-west roads converge. Situated in the heart of a fertile region and thanks to a highly efficient irrigation system, Granadilla is now a key agricultural centre. Vines, tomatoes, potatoes and oranges proliferate around the town. Granadilla has extended southwards and some smallish industrial concerns have moved here. It is the most populated town in the south of Tenerife, but it is a working town and there is not much here of interest to the tourist, apart from a small Baroque church in the centre and a number of squares.

Paisaje Lunar (C5)

★ About 20 km from Vilaflor, hidden away on the edge of the Cañadas lies the Paisaje Lunar or 'Lunar Landscape'. Above the village, on a right-hand bend near km marker 66, a forest track signposted *Palo Blanco* begins. This bumpy 7-km lane passes one or two isolated farmsteads and ends at the Camp Fuente Madre del Agua. Leave your car and follow the footpath that leads round the camp. When you reach a tight curve, leave the path and turn left through a damp gorge. Continue on as far as a narrow ridge that leads upwards, towards the group of large rocks you'll see up ahead. After about 50 m, the path forks and you will see a water pipe leading down the valley into a *barranco*. Take the uphill route to the right of the water pipe. Follow the small gorge to the left and you will eventually reach a plateau. The view over Vilaflor and the terraced hillsides is breathtaking. Carry on into the woods where the terrain becomes easier. A wide hollow comes into view as bizarre tufa rock formations of towers and turrets gleam in the sun.

Poris de Abona (E5)

This little fishing village lies to the south of Arico. A neat but rather humdrum holiday village has been built on its outskirts. Two small, rocky beaches are suitable for swimming, and sunworshippers can lie alongside the fishing boats to soak up the rays.

Vilaflor (C5)

★ Seven kilometres north-west of Granadilla de Abona, on the road from south Tenerife to the Caldera de las Cañadas, sits the highest inhabited settlement on the island. At 1400 m, the village of Vilaflor (pop. 1500) is surrounded by balsamic pine forests in the north and terraced hillsides and fields in the south. The woodland micro-climate and the clear air at this altitude are very beneficial to those who suffer from lung disorders.

Enjoy the crisp, clean air of Vilaflor

Visitors to Vilaflor will find a quiet, neat little hamlet where time seems to have stood still. Most tourists come here because it is an ideal point of departure for hikes in the Caldera de las Cañadas. There is a small factory nearby that bottles spring-water, which is distributed throughout the island. Just outside Vilaflor stand two huge pine trees, one 42 m, the other 53 m tall, both 4 m in diameter. Viewing platforms have been built around the trunks of these wonderful giants. But for a truly stunning panorama, take the road to the viewing platform ◁▷ *Mirador de San Roque* which is signposted from Vilaflor. The view from here encompasses the surrounding countryside, including the peaceful little coastal spa of El Médano. A small chapel lies hidden among the pine trees.

Vilaflor is renowned for its lace, which can be bought directly from family-run shops. The church in the upper village is dedicated to San Pedro, the missionary and travelling priest known as Hermano Pedro (Brother Peter), who was born in Vilaflor and constructed the chapel himself in 1550.

The great holiday playground

A haven for beach-lovers and watersports enthusiasts

The southern tip of the island is dominated by the major tourist resort of Playa de las Américas, a town hewn from the bare rock and laid out in chequer-board style, joining almost seamlessly with the twin resort of Los Cristianos. If you enjoy scenic views and green landscapes, then this part of Tenerife is not the place for you. The only vegetation in these parts are the banana plantations, many situated close to the numerous holiday developments and hotels. To compensate, this flat coastal region is ideal for windsurfers and other watersports fans. But if you want to get to know the people and experience something of their everyday lifestyle, you will have to go further afield and explore the villages that line the coast, such as La Caleta, Abama, San Juan, Alcalá and Puerto de Santiago. This stretch of the shoreline is dotted with small beaches and quiet fishing alcoves.

Stark mountains surround the modern tourist mecca of Playa de las Americas

LOS CRISTIANOS

(C6) This busy town overlooking a broad bay has two faces. The old fishing village has largely been engulfed by sprawling hotels and apartment blocks. Many of the locals, the majority of whom come from exceedingly modest backgrounds, have been lured into the opportunistic mood that seized Playa de las Américas.

The bay is surrounded by a promenade and a wide, white sandy beach, where tourists from chilly northern climes flock to laze around in the sun. At the bay's southern end, a reddish crag juts out into the sea and the bay finishes abruptly in front of a desert of scree. Flowers bloom in gardens surrounding the holiday resorts, and young roadside trees offer welcome respite from the blistering sun. A pedestrian zone lined with cafés, restaurants and shops leads to the plaza on the edge of the town. Narrow streets leading toward the harbour retain some of the original traits of this old fishing town. Take the time to seek out a higher vantage point for a splendid view of the harbour, and when the ferry or hydrofoil from Gomera steams in, watch the port suddenly teem with life. Light craft, some of which have been converted into 'pirate ships', ply the coastline and yachts both large and small weigh anchor alongside fishing boats and pedalos. Overlooking the resort, modern terraced houses cling to the volcanic Chayofita. Behind the breakwater, a pretty promenade leads onto Playa de las Américas.

SIGHTS

Cactus Park - Tenerife Zoo
This natural parkland holds the largest cactus collection in the world with over 1000 species of cactus and desert plant. Four kilometres away from Los Cristianos, this 100-hectare site provides the perfect arid conditions for these plants to thrive in. Visitors are offered an informative brochure providing detailed descriptions of the plants' life-cycles, individual characteristics and natural environments.

Annexed to the Cactus Park is a small zoo that keeps various members of the cat family; some species of monkey have also been introduced recently. Of particular interest is a section called 'Amazonia' where colourful hummingbirds and butterflies flit among the tropical plants and flowers. Other creatures that inhabit the zoo include a variety of birds, insects, iguanas and all sorts of reptiles.

To get here by car, leave the motorway at the Valle San Lorenzo exit. The entrance to the park is about 200 m higher up

(signposted). All of the nearby tourist resorts offer free bus services to the park.
Daily 09.30-18.00 hrs; Entrance to Cactus Park/Amazonia for adults 1250 ptas, Tenerife Zoo only, 400 ptas, children 400 ptas

Jardines del Atlántico/Bananera
Visitors to this oasis can learn about the island's plant life, how the islanders live and how water is collected. There is a guided tour through a banana plantation and a small exhibition of typical Canarian farming tools. Most hotel reception desks, tour operators and travel agents will supply information about the times of the free buses from Los Cristianos and Playa de las Américas.
Entrance: 750 ptas

RESTAURANTS

Golden Curry
For a change from Canarian cuisine, this restaurant offers a wide selection of Indian food. It is conveniently located in the San Telmo shopping centre.
Daily 13.00-16.00 and 18.00-00.30 hrs; San Telmo Center; Tel: 908 10 59 10; Category 3

Casa del Mar
〰 Restaurant by the harbour with a wide selection of fresh fish.
Daily from 18.00 hrs; Category 2

El Sol Chez Jacques
French-style restaurant-bistro.
Daily 13.00-15.00 and 19.00-23.00 hrs; Between C/. General Franco and C/. Juan XXIII; Category 2

Swiss Chalet
A restaurant specializing in typical Swiss dishes, offering 12

different types of fondues.
Daily (except Wednesday) from 18.00 hrs; Avda. Suecia; Category 1

SHOPPING

Juan XXIII Pedestrianized Zone

This lively area with its countless little shops and boutiques is closed to traffic and makes for an enjoyable shopping spree.

HOTELS

The majority of hotels, apartments and tourist complexes in Los Cristianos fall in the three-star category, but a few luxury hotels have recently appeared. Cheaper accommodation can be found in the old town where there are a number of small pensions, mostly frequented by English, German or Scandinavian tourists.

Gran Hotel Arona

A four-star hotel by the bay.
400 rooms; Tel: 75 06 78, Fax: 75 02 43; Category 1

Marysol

Apartment complex with facilities for disabled guests. Physiotherapy treatments also available. About 700 m from the beach.
115 rooms; Tel: 75 05 40, Fax: 79 54 73; Category 2

Paradise Park

New apartment complex with attractive garden and plenty of organized activities on offer.
280 rooms; Tel: 79 60 11, Fax: 79 84 59; Category 2

MARCO POLO SELECTION: THE SOUTH-WEST COAST

1 Las Aguilas del Teide
Wildlife park overlooking Los Cristianos, featuring a wide range of tropical flora and birds of prey (page 79)

2 El Médano
Once a little fishing and farming village, this is the only place on the island with naturally light-coloured sand (page 77)

3 Cueva del Hermano Pedro
A remarkable cave near El Médano (page 78)

4 Barranco del Infierno
Take a walk along this desolate 'devil's gorge' and admire the 80-m high waterfall (page 82)

5 Playa de la Arena
A delightful beach in Puerto de Santiago (page 84)

6 Playa de Santiago
Black sand beach at the foot of the towering Los Gigantes cliff (page 83)

7 A diving trip
Marvel at the wonders of the deep from a submarine off the Costa del Silencio near Las Galletas (page 77)

8 Pastas a Go Go
A restaurant in Playa de las Américas serving 99 different pasta dishes (page 79)

9 El Patio
A luxury restaurant in Playa de las Américas (page 79)

Los Cristianos harbour

Princesa Dacil
This is the biggest hotel in Los Cristianos. It has large gardens and a swimming pool. The rooms are well-equipped and there is a wide range of entertainment on offer. About 500 m from the beach.
366 rooms; Camino Penetración; Tel: 79 08 00, Fax: 79 06 58; Category 2

Tenerife-Sur
Comfortable apartments with restaurant, bar, sauna and squash. 500 m from the sea.
189 rooms; Tel: 79 14 74, Fax: 79 27 74; Category 2

Pensión La Paloma
Small family-run pension not far from the port. Modest rooms.
Corner C/. Juan XXIII; Tel: 79 01 98

SPORT & LEISURE

✻ Enthusiasts can make reservations for shark fishing expeditions, boat trips along the coast in the 'Pirate Ship' and rent pedalos in the harbour. Water sports fans need only go to the beach to hire equipment for windsurfing, sports accessories, speedboats, waterskiing and parasailing.

Karting Club Tenerife
✻ This extensive go-kart track is situated near the motorway between Los Cristianos and Playa de las Américas. Also suitable for families with children.

Deep-sea fishing
✻ For anglers, a range of boats are available for hire in Los Cristianos harbour.

ENTERTAINMENT

Casablanca
Comfortable and relaxing piano bar located on the upper floor of the shopping centre by the San Telmo promenade.
Entrance via staircase.

Dream Palace
✻ This mega-disco features live shows.
Daily from 22.00 hrs, above Los Cristianos near the Cactus Park

La Roca
Open-air disco with live shows and guest appearances.
Daily from 20.00 hrs, on the rock at the end of the promenade

Policía Municipal
Tel: 72 51 00

Guardia Civil
Tel: 79 14 14

SURROUNDING AREA

Las Galletas (C6)

The Costa del Silencio ('Coast of Silence') is the Spanish name for this section of coast at the southernmost tip of the island, a few kilometres west of the Reina Sofía Airport. It is a rocky coastline with no sandy beaches, just the odd cove with steps down to the sea. The green hills along the coast are dotted with holiday developments built around Las Galletas, a small fishing port at the southern tip of the island. It became a busy tourist centre after the opening of Tenbel, a French-style holiday village to the north of the town. Tenbel stands for Tenerife-Belgium as it was a Belgian company that made the initial investment. Not surprisingly, it is very popular with Belgian holidaymakers. The complex offers differing types of accommodation, mostly apartments and bungalows. Surrounded by a tropical garden with several swimming pools, Tenbel offers a wide variety of sporting and recreational facilities *(Tel: 78 58 15; Category 2)*. The prosperity this new development has brought to Las Galletas is reflected in the many modern buildings that have sprung up around its outskirts. The fishing village, which now has small shops, cafés and restaurants, has blossomed into an attractive and friendly resort.

A small promenade runs along the seafront, and a bathing beach where fishing boats anchor lies to the west. This is a good spot for windsurfing and hire boards are available by the beach. ★ For a novel experience why not explore the underwater world aboard the Finnish submarine *Subtrek*. Free bus services run between Las Galletas, Playa de las Américas, Los Cristianos and Playa de la Cruz.

To the north-east of Las Galletas, set in the midst of banana plantations and other tropical plants, is the Nauta camping and caravan site which offers all the usual facilities *(Camping- and Caravan- Club Nauta, Las Galletas, Cañada Blanca; Tel: 78 59 71, 78 51 18)*.

El Médano (D6)

★ ☆ Not so long ago, El Médano was just a quiet fishing and farming community (pop. 1000), but in recent years it has been transformed into a major tourist centre. Situated near the Reina Sofía Airport, at the foot of Montaña Roja, this village boasts the longest and finest sandy beach on the island. Stretching to almost 3 km, it is Tenerife's only naturally light sand beach. It is lined with hotels, small apartment blocks and a campsite. It is also considered a windsurfer's paradise and has been selected on a number of occasions as a site for international windsurfing competitions. The beach extends from both sides of Montaña Roja, a 171 m volcanic cone. The western side is better for swimming and sunbathing, but windsurfers prefer the eastern side, as the constant on-shore breezes provide the ideal climatic conditions for this popular watersport. But El Médano is not just for windsurfers. Non-surfers appreciate this little resort for its peaceful setting and idyllic, romantic atmosphere. Asthmatics and those who suffer from rheumatic and allergic complaints find that the climate here can be very beneficial to their health. In the village, behind the pretty square, is a busy beach, popular with families, that is sheltered from the sea breeze by the surrounding hotels. Magellan is said to have moored here in 1519 while in the service of the Spanish king.

Despite the influx of tourism, however, El Médano is still a relatively calm and peaceful resort and retains something of its original character. The port is predominantly filled with fishing boats and many of the original narrow streets, alleys and houses remain intact. Along the short promenade, around the square and in the village, there are numerous comfortable restaurants and cafés with terraces. In the evenings, holidaymakers and locals congregate in the bars, pubs and small discotheques near the square and it is easy to meet new friends. Hungry holidaymakers in El Médano should pay a visit to the Avencio restaurant, where fish and shellfish are specialities *(Daily from 13.00 hrs; Opposite the plaza; Category 2).*

Good accommodation is offered by the family-run Playa Sur Tenerife hotel. It is situated close to the beach and has a swimming pool and garden. Cars, bicycles and boards can be hired at the hotel and board transportation is also available. Guests can opt for a room with breakfast or half-board.

There is also a windsurfing school annexed to the hotel *(Tel: 17 60 13, 17 61 21; Category 2).*

Further west of the Playa Sur Tenerife hotel is the ★ *Cueva del Hermano Pedro.* To reach this cave, follow the signposted path for about 200 m until you reach a turn-off on the right. The grotto lies about 500 m down this path. Hermano Pedro (Brother Pedro) was a missionary who founded an order of monks in Brazil, which later spread throughout central America. He tried to introduce Christianity to Tenerife, but without much success. He was even chased out of Vilaflor where he had built the church of San Pedro in 1550. This cave, which has been named after him, was his final refuge. He was canonized some years ago and twice a year a mass is celebrated in the cave in his honour.

San Miguel (C5)

Situated between Granadilla and Valle de San Lorenzo, San Miguel remains an unspoilt village. It is known for its lovely flower gardens and orange groves, as well as for Juan Bethancourt Alfonso, a famous physician and a historian of the Canary Islands who was born here. His birthplace lies to the right of the church. Beneath San Miguel stands the Castillo San Miguel, a replica castle where medieval jousting contests are held. Ask at the travel agent for further information.

PLAYA DE LAS AMÉRICAS

(C6) Playa de la Américas is a completely artificial resort that is only

30 years old. The huge hotel and apartment complex was built on a flat, 5-km strip along the sunny south-west coast of Tenerife. In the early 1960s, this part of the island was a sandy, stony desert, brightened by a few banana plantations. When the planners set to work, they decided to relieve what would be large expanses of concrete by filling the spaces between the hotels and villas with spacious gardens and by planting palm trees along the roadsides. Construction continues, in an effort to accommodate the ever increasing numbers of tourists.

Swimming and sunbathing on the Playa de las Américas is limited to three small dark sand beaches, and if you're here during the high season you'll need to arrive early in order to stake out your patch of sand. To help alleviate congestion, a new beach called Las Vistas is being created between Playa de las Américas and Los Cristianos, along with a marina.

The nightlife here is pretty lively and the countless bars, pubs and discos are buzzing until the early hours. Walkers enjoy the long promenade that follows the coast round to Los Cristianos. This part of Tenerife is not so much the 'Island of Eternal Spring' as the 'Island of Eternal Summer'.

SIGHTS

Las Águilas del Teide
★ Tropical flora flourish in this wildlife park, but the real crowd pullers are the birds of prey. These magnificent creatures can be seen performing several times a day, while in the evening, the nocturnal birds are the star attraction, as they provide unusual en-tertainment at the gala dinners held here. Free bus services are available between all the major tourist centres and the park.
Daily 10.00-18.00 hrs; Entrance 2000 ptas

RESTAURANTS

The Galleon
Popular steakhouse in the Royal Gardens Centre. Wide choice of dishes; children accompanied by adults dine free.
Daily 12.00-15.00 and 19.00-24.00 hrs; Playa de las Américas; Tel: 75 16 63; Category 2

Da Angelo
Comfortable Italian restaurant serving home-made specialities, all prepared by the proprietress.
Daily from 13.00 hrs; Costa Torviscas shopping centre; Category 2

La Karina
Superior café-restaurant with a fine terrace.
Daily from 10.00 hrs; in the main street below the Hotel Sol; Category 2

Pastas a Go Go
★ Well-run restaurant by the Puerto Colón marina. Ninety-nine pasta dishes on the menu, all home-made. Good selection of Italian and Spanish wines.
Daily (except Tuesday) 12.00-24.00 hrs; Puerto Colón shopping centre; Category 2

El Patio
★ Restaurant/piano-bar in the Jardín Tropical Hotel, set out like a typical Canarian patio. Bags of atmosphere and an international menu.
Daily 13.00-16.00 and 19.00-24.00 hrs; By the promenade; Category 1

SHOPPING

Centro América Shopping
Small, specialist shops and market stalls selling beachwear, perfume, cosmetics and souvenirs. Also has a number of restaurants, cafés and bars.
Near the Hotel Las Palmeras

City Center
Specialist shops on two floors, selling textiles, jewellery, clocks, watches, cameras and embroidery. Also has restaurants, cafés and bars.
Between Los Cardones and La Siesta hotels.

Santiago III
Smart shopping centre set on several floors in apartment complex of the same name. All sorts of shops with numerous restaurants and bars.
Open throughout the day

Shopping Center Bougainville
Good quality shops and a variety of market stalls. This is the place for those wanting to buy cameras and photographic equipment, electronic goods, leather goods, jewellery, clocks, watches, perfume and beachwear. If you're looking for books, magazines and newspapers, head to the Bougan Shop.
Below the Bougainville Hotel

HOTELS

Playa de las Américas is principally made up of large, modern holiday apartment blocks and villas. The decor in the more luxurious hotels is characterized by gleaming marble inside and lush greenery outside, generally featuring large swimming pools surrounded by exotic plants.

Gran Hotel Bahía del Duque
Top-grade luxury hotel, designed like a Canarian village. Good range of sport and leisure facilities, suites, conference halls, several restaurants and bars.
362 rooms; Fañabé district; Tel: 71 30 00, Fax: 71 26 16; Category 1

Gala
New four-star hotel right by the beach.
Tel: 79 46 00, Fax: 79 64 65; Category 2

Jardín Tropical
Moorish-style hotel set in the middle of a lush tropical garden. Includes a sports and fitness centre. Restaurant and bar.
427 rooms; San Eugenio district; Tel: 75 01 00, 79 51 11, Fax: 75 28 44; Category 1

Hotel Vulcano
Well-run modern 4-star hotel with a beautifully landscaped garden. Near the beach.
450 rooms; Avda. Antonio Domínguez, 6; Tel: 79 20 35, Fax: 79 28 53; Category 1

Pueblo Torviscas
Villas and apartments by the Playa de Torviscas. 'Aparthotels' also available.
185 rooms; Tel: 79 06 90, Fax: 75 20 51; Category 2

SPORT & LEISURE

Swimming
Aguapark Octopus
This leisure pool on the edge of town features several swimming pools, waterslides and watercourses. An aquatic paradise for

children and the young at heart.
Entrance for adults: 2000 ptas, entrance free for children under 11; with bus service from Puerto de la Cruz 2900 ptas

The coastline around Playa de las Américas is comprised mainly of white sandy beaches, interspersed with occasional stretches of dark sand and interrupted only by breakwaters. Playa de Troya and Playa del Bobo are probably the best beaches, as they have fine sand. Also recommended is the beach near the new marina at Puerto Colón at the western end of the promenade, which is small but pretty.

Boat hire
Motor boats and pedalos can be hired at the Puerto Colón marina.

Parasailing
On the Playa de Troya.

Jeep safaris
⚑ A jeep safari is by far the best way to explore the island's interior. The dense forest and volcanic terrain are difficult to cross on foot or in an ordinary hire car, but in a four-wheel drive, a cross-country journey becomes a real adventure. Prices vary depending on the route you opt for and the meals provided. Your hotel should be able to recommend a reputable company, but before booking make sure that the organization you select is fully insured.

Sailing
Boats can be hired in the marina. Be sure to check the condition of the vessel before setting off and verify that all the safety fittings are functioning.

Squash
There are squash courts at the Conquistador and Europe hotels.

Diving
There are some interesting dive sites around the island and it's not a bad place to learn either. Enquire at the Poseidon Nemrod diving school in the Hotel Las Palmeras *(Tel: 79 09 91)*, at the Baracuda Diving and Windsurfing Club in the Hotel Paraíso Floral in Adeje *(Tel: 78 07 25)* and the Diving and Windsurfing school in the Hotel Oasis Paraíso *(Tel: 78 10 51)*.

Tennis
Almost all the hotels on the island are equipped with tennis courts; a number of them are even floodlit at night. Tennis coaches are sometimes available for private lessons.

Walking
Day-long hikes are organized by the Innsbruck Alpine Walking School (enquire at the *Hotel Park Club Europe; Tel: 79 29 70*) as well as by TIMAH – a mountain walkers group. *Tel: 71 02 42.*

Waterskiing and speedboats
At the Puerto Colón marina and Playa de Troya beach.

Windsurfing
Boards for hire on the Playa de Troya beach.

ENTERTAINMENT

Bananas Garden
Disco pub with terrace in the centre of Playa de las Américas, opposite the beach.
Daily 12.00 hrs until late

Exit 29
Mega-disco in the upper San Eugenio district.
Daily from 22.00 hrs

Night-Club Melodies
Friendly nightclub with shows and live music. Join in and dance or just listen.
Daily from 22.00 hrs; in the Poderosa apartment complex

Memphis
For jazz fans. Regular changes to the programme.
Daily from 22.00 hrs; Lagos de Fañabé, Playa de Tòrviscas

INFORMATION

Oficinas de Turismo
Daily 09.00-16.00 hrs; Urb. Tòrviscas, opposite Hotel La Pinta; Tel: 75 03 66, Fax: 75 20 32
Daily 09.00-15.30 hrs; City Centre; Tel: 79 76 68

SURROUNDING AREA

Adeje   (C5)
Although encircled by modern buildings, the centre of Adeje (pop. 2500) is a quiet spot whose steep main street is lined with whitewashed houses, cafés and laurel trees. Before the Spanish conquest, Adeje was the seat of the Guanche kings – the Menceys – and a Guanche shrine was situated at the nearby Roque del Conde. When the Guanches yielded to the Spaniards, Adeje became the seat of a noble lord, whose family retained control of the town until 1840. The only vestiges of this feudal period are found in the area around the 16th-century Santa Úrsula church, some 17th-century houses and the 16th-century Casa Fuerte at the edge of the town. The Casa Fuerte, outside of which stands an ornate cannon, is now used as a banana packaging warehouse. The church itself contains priceless, late 17th-century Gobelins tapestries, which hang near the choir stalls. The altarpiece, which was made for the counts of Gomera, features a number of simple renderings of the island's patron saints. There are two balconies in the apse that were originally reserved for nobility, who were protected from the congregation's gaze by a grid.

One of Tenerife's most popular destinations for walkers is the scenic ★ *Barranco del Infierno* (Devil's Gorge) which features a dramatic waterfall and is found on the north-east of Adeje. It can be reached by taking the path that joins the church of Santa Ursula to the Casa Fuerte. Follow the path until you reach a car park on the left-hand side. A sign marked *Barranco del Infierno* points to the recently-renovated trail that leads into the gorge. The route winds its way along the *barranco* and initially the going is quite easy, but the further you proceed, the stonier the path becomes, so sturdy shoes are essential. At first the vegetation is sparse, but as you penetrate into the gorge it becomes more dense and lush. One of the first landmarks is the *'Bailadero de las Brujas'* ('Where the witches dance'). The view from here is quite stunning. You will eventually come to a sharp bend, around which the end of the gorge comes into view. A little further on you will see the water trickling from the 80 m-high waterfall. Water only flows down the *barranco* during the winter months or after a rainy period. Occasionally, after a very wet spell, the stream that runs alongside the path overflows, making the route impassable, but otherwise it is not an arduous journey and you don't have to be an ex-

Holiday village in Los Gigantes

perienced hiker to undertake it. Allow about four hours for the excursion there and back.

La Caleta (B-C 6)
La Caleta is a tiny fishing village, as yet unspoilt by tourism. The sea is clear and calm, but you have to clamber over the shoreline rocks to reach it. Recommended restaurants: the Cala Marín, which serves fresh fish and seafood *(Category 2)*, and the Celso *(Category 2)*.

Los Gigantes (B5)
This seaside village owes its name to the truly gigantic 500 m-high rocks, which rise sharply out of the sea. These cliffs mark the abrupt end to the Teno hills and the beginning of a flat coastal strip. Los Gigantes now consists almost entirely of modern apartments, villas and some largish ho-

tels. The road winds its way down to the marina and to the adjoining black sand ★ Playa de Santiago at the foot of the cliffs. Only a few of the village's original buildings remain and most of these have been converted or renovated. Designed to blend in with the natural surroundings, the Santiago is the largest hotel, with 382 beds, extensive lawns, a large pool and plenty of entertainment laid on for guests *(Category 1)*.

Guía de Isora (B5)
This little town lies at about 600 m above sea level in a barren lava landscape. A good supply of water has helped to create the right conditions for fruit and vegetable production and much of the surrounding land consists of terraces where tomatoes and potatoes are cultivated. Almond trees are also grown in this region. The church of the Virgen de la Luz by the square, renovated during the 1950s, is worth a quick visit for the statue of the Virgin by Lujan Perez, among other interesting works. Guía de Isora is a good base from which to explore the villages of Aripe and Chirche and the Barranco de Tágara.

Puerto de Santiago (B5)
This fishing village is now encircled by villas and apartment blocks. It is a more up-market resort which, despite the influx of tourists, still retains its individual character. The *Tamaimo Tropical Aparthotel* offers one or two bedroom apartments, a restaurant, bar, two swimming pools, a solarium with jacuzzi and tennis courts *(200 rooms; Tel: 10 06 38, Fax: 10 07 61; Category 2)*. Also recommended is the *Apartamentos*

Punta Negra complex by the coast *(14 apartments only, Category 2)*.

Above the pretty ★ Playa de la Arena, a small open area dotted with benches provides a fine view of the beach, the sea and the island of Gomera in the distance. The *La Sirena* beach restaurant offers both refreshments and meals. The fish and grilled specialities are highly recommended. Over supper you can listen to live music and watch the sunset. Further up is a small promenade lined with bars, restaurants, market stalls, a bank and a bureau de change with telephone kiosks.

San Juan   (B5)

There's always a lively atmosphere in this busy fishing village. The catch is unloaded early in the morning and much of it will be found on the menus of the nearby restaurants. You can swim by the harbour or off the rocky shore, and fish from the breakwater. *La Historía de Don José* is a popular bar-restaurant that serves meat specialities and freshly-caught fish *(Category 3)*.

NEIGHBOURING ISLANDS

Gomera

An airport is under construction on the island, and it will soon be accessible by plane. At the moment it can only be reached by ferry. There are four crossings per day between Los Cristianos and San Sebastián and the journey takes about 90 minutes.

Gomera (pop. 16 000) covers an area of 378 sq. km. The interior is cut through with numerous *barrancos* which widen out nearer the coast. The hilly terrain is sprinkled with villages and hamlets. It may look like a barren wasteland from a distance, but in fact the interior is verdant and fertile. The centre of the island is now the Garajonay National Park, a jungle of green where thick forest alternates with dense shrubs. This protected area lies to the north of the island's highest peak, the 1487-m high ☙ Garajonay. The stunning view from the top of this mountain encompasses the whole of Gomera and the neighbouring islands. On a clear day, the Pico del Teide, some 60 km away, is clearly visible. Water is plentiful and Canarian palm trees flourish in the lower coastal regions. In the south and east, the vegetation is sparser as there is comparatively little rainfall. In the north, the soil is rich and fertile, the rainfall plentiful, and there are effective irrigation sytems in place. These are optimum conditions for the cultivation of sub-tropical and tropical fruits, such as bananas, avocados, mangoes and pawpaws. Fishing also plays an important role in the local economy and there are two canning and processing factories on the island.

The main town is San Sebastián de la Gomera on the east coast (pop. 5600). Christopher Columbus called in here several times to replenish his vessels' water tanks. Hermigua, the second-largest settlement on the island, lies a few kilometres inland and is surrounded by banana plantations. Los Órganos on the far northern tip of the island is a 200-m wide rock formation consisting of 80-m high basalt columns, lined up like church organ pipes. But by far the best place to visit on the island is the Valle Gran Rey in the west. This lush valley lies between two gorges and its terraced hillsides are filled with palm groves and banana plantations.

Good accommodation is provided in the *Conde de la Gomera Parador Nacional* in San Sebastián *(42 rooms; Tel: 87 11 00, Fax: 87 11 16; Category 1)*. The biggest hotel is the ☙ *Tecina* above *Playa de Santiago (342 rooms; Tel: 89 50 50; Category 1)*, which enjoys a splendid panoramic view. *La Laguna Grande* restaurant in the Garajonay National Park *(Category 2)* serves good food. The tender grilled meat dishes and tuna fish steaks are particularly delicious.

Hierro

Hierro (277 sq. km, pop. 7100) is the smallest of the Canary Islands. The quickest way to reach it is by plane from Los Rodeos airport, although the half-hour flight is often cancelled because of adverse winds. Alternatively a regular ferry service operates between Los Cristianos and Puerto de la Estaca. Valverde (pop. 2000) in the north-east is the main town. It is a mountainous island dominated by Malpaso (1500 m), a mountain covered in sparse, green vegetation. Forestry and farming are the main source of employment as tourism has not had much of an impact yet. There is some attractive scenery (such as El Golfo bay), but few beaches. The El Hierro Parador Nacional in Valverde is the main hotel on the island *(47 rooms; Tel: 55 80 36, Fax: 55 80 86; Category 1)*. The restaurant specializing in seafood and local stews is excellent.

El Golfo bay lies at the foot of Hierro's central mountain range on the island's north-west coast

Practical information

Important addresses and useful information
for your visit to Tenerife

AIRPORTS

There are two airports in Tenerife: Los Rodeos near Santa Cruz in the north is for inter-island and domestic flights *(Tel: 25 79 40)*, while Reina Sofía just outside El Médano in the south is for international flights *(Tel: 77 00 50)*.

BANKS & MONEY

Banks are open every day from 09.00 to 14.00 hrs. They usually close on Saturdays during the summer months. Eurocheques are widely accepted and should be made out in pesetas. The maximum amount per cheque is 30 000 ptas. If you want to change cash, the bureau de change rates are generally more favourable, but it is worth enquiring first about the charges and commissions, as they vary greatly. It's also possible to change money in travel agencies and at the reception desks of the larger hotels. The unit of currency is the peseta

Ten minutes in a cable car is
all it takes to reach the top of
Pico del Teide

(pta). Coins come in denominations of 1, 5, 10, 25, 50, 100, 200 and 500 pesetas and there are banknotes of 1000, 2000, 5000 and 10 000 pesetas (see page 96 for current exchange rates).

BEACHES

Most of the light-coloured sandy beaches on Tenerife are concentrated in the south of the island. If you see a red flag flying, it means that it's too dangerous to swim. Not all beaches are supervised so, as a general rule, it's advisable to follow the locals' lead – they know the safest places to swim.

BOAT TRIPS

To Gomera
There are four car ferry sailings per day between Gomera and Los Cristianos. The crossing takes about 90 minutes. Departures from Los Cristianos are at 09.00, 12.30, 16.00 and 20.00 hrs and from San Sebastián de la Gomera at 07.00, 10.45, 14.15 and 18.00 hrs. The single fare for one person is 1850 ptas and 3000 ptas for a mid-range saloon car. The

'Barracuda' hydrofoil only takes 35 minutes but is more expensive (return fare 5000 ptas). Departures from Los Cristianos 09.00, 12.30, 16.00 and 18.00 hrs, San Sebastián 08.00, 10.15, 14.00 and 17.00 hrs.

To Gran Canaria
A jetfoil links Santa Cruz de Tenerife with Las Palmas de Gran Canaria. The crossing takes about 80 minutes and costs 5531 ptas. There is also a jetfoil service to Fuerteventura that operates on Monday, Wednesday and Friday. Another car ferry runs between Santa Cruz and Agaete on the west coast of Gran Canaria. There are four sailings every day in both directions and the crossing takes about 2 hours. The fare for a single journey is 2876 ptas per person; a medium-sized saloon car costs 9427 ptas.

BUSES

The local bus company (TITSA) operates a network of services which cover the whole island. Timetables are available from bus stations and TITSA booths. Bus stops are indicated by roadside signs. If you're planning on using the buses frequently it's worth looking into the 'Bono-Bus' multiple-ticket system which will save you money. The Santa Cruz bus station is on the Avenida Tres de Mayo (by the motorway exit). The station in Puerto de la Cruz is situated in the Poligono centre (behind the old town). In Playa de las Américas, the buses depart from Pueblo Canario opposite the Gran Tinerfe hotel and in Los Cristianos they leave from the central taxi rank.

CAMPING

There is only one official campsite in the south of the island: *Camping Nauta, Cañada Blanca/ Las Galletas; Tel: 78 51 18.*

Camping in the wild on the coast between El Médano and Los Abrigos, in Bajamar/Punta del Hidalgo and near Puerto de Güímar is tolerated. If you wish to camp in the National Park, however, you should seek prior permission from the ICONA environmental protection authorities (*Avda. de Anaga 35, Santa Cruz de Tenerife; Tel: 33 07 01*).

There are no official campsites on Gomera or Hierro.

CAR HIRE

There is a wide range of car rental offices in all the major resorts on Tenerife and at both airports, and vehicles of every size and make are available. It is definitely worth taking the time to compare prices as they vary widely in this competitive business. Rates include unlimited mileage. You will be asked to show your national driving licence. Alternatively, you can book a hire car prior to your departure. Ask your travel agent for details.

CHEMISTS

A sign with a green cross against a white background indicates a chemist (*farmacia*). They are usually open from Monday to Friday 09.00–13.00 and 16.00–19.00 hrs and on Saturday morning until 13.00 hrs. The addresses of emergency chemists (*farmacia de guardia*) are displayed in every chemist shop window.

CONSULATES

United Kingdom
Calle de Suárez Guerra 40 (5th floor)
Santa Cruz de Tenerife
Tel: 24 20 00

Edificio Cataluña
Calle de Luis Morote 6 (3rd floor)
Las Palmas de Gran Canaria
Tel: 26 25 08

United States
Calle José Franchy Roca 5
Las Palmas de Gran Canaria
Tel: 27 12 59

CREDIT CARDS

In the event of a lost or stolen credit card, contact:
American Express
Tel: 91/459 90 09
Diners Club
Tel: 91/247 40 00
Eurocheque
Tel: 07/49/69/74 09 87
Visa
Tel: 91/435 24 45

CUSTOMS

From a customs point of view, Tenerife is not part of the EU and therefore some restrictions apply to exported goods. Only 2 litres of wine or 1 1itre of spirits, 200 cigarettes or 100 cigarillos or 50 cigars may be taken home. You may be told on the island that it is legal to take home larger quantities. This is not the case, but visitors to other EU countries from Spain, or the Canary Islands, are not usually subject to customs checks.

DOCTORS

All members of EU countries are entitled to free medical treatment. An E111 form (obtainable by British nationals from the social security office) should, in theory, cover treatment expenses, but not prescriptions. It is nevertheless advisable to take out a temporary private medical insurance as this will protect you against all eventualities and reduce bureaucratic delays.

The following medical centres provide a 24-hour emergency service:
Centro Medico Dr Juan Ruiz Garcia,
Plaza del Charco 6
Puerto de la Cruz
Tel: 38 11 11

Safer driving

One habit that local drivers adopt is to let the left arm dangle casually from the car window. It's worth keeping an eye on this arm as if it starts to move then it indicates a situation of potential danger. The more agitated the arm, the more hazardous the situation. So don't just watch for the brake lights of the car in front, which are often not easy to pick out in the bright sunlight. The important thing is to be ready to brake. You do not have to dangle your left arm and the practice is not a part of the Spanish highway code, but it is something that most car drivers do and it could prevent a bump or a lot of hassle.

Centro Médico Internacional,
Pueblo Canario,
Playa de las Américas
Tel: 79 17 11

The National Police *(Policía Nacional)* are responsible for security and traffic. *Tel: 091* (only in Santa Cruz, La Laguna and Puerto de la Cruz).

Local police *(Policía Municipal)*, Santa Cruz de Tenerife; *Tel: 092;* Puerto de la Cruz, *C/. Santo Domingo; Tel: 38 12 24;* Playa de las Américas, Pueblo Canario; *Tel: 76 51 00*

Criminal police *(Guardia Civil); Tel: 22 11 00*

INFORMATION

Useful information for your holiday can be obtained from the Spanish Tourist Office:

United Kingdom
57-58 St James's Street
London SW1A 1LD

United States
665 Fifth Avenue
New York NY 10022
Tel: (112) 759 88 22

Tenerife
Palacio Insular
Plaza de España
Santa Cruz
Tel: 24 20 90

Plaza de la Iglesia 3
Puerto de la Cruz
Tel: 38 60 00

NEWSPAPERS

English newspapers usually arrive on Tenerife the day after publication. You can also pick up the *International Herald Tribune* here.

PASSPORTS

Visitors from the UK and the USA must carry a current passport. No visa is required for a stay of up to three months.

PICNIC SITES (ZONAS RECREATIVAS)

❖ Most picnic sites are located in wooded areas and equipped with barbecue grills, benches and sometimes even running water. Many have children's playgrounds too. Firewood, often chopped and stored in a pile, is usually provided. Locals often picnic in the *chozas*, which are

---

The Eighth Canary

Truth or fiction? The notion of a lost Canary Island has long captured the popular imagination, resulting in epithets as evocative as they are inevitable: the landscapes of this paradise were (of course) magical, with crystalline streams, ancient trees, crimson blossoms and tame wildlife. Prosperity reigned and food was abundant. One had only to reach out to pick succulent fruit or to haul in a net miraculouly filled with fish. Many sailors claim to have seen it, but say that the island vanished upon their approach. The myth is no doubt rooted in a volcanic phenomenon that rose from the sea, only to be resubmerged.

---

wayside shelters. *Zonas Recreativas* are found in the scenic areas or popular walking regions. In the summer, the Tinerfiños love to leave the towns for the cool shade of the forests and then the picnic sites become overcrowded and barbecue grills are at a premium. The solution is to arrive early.

La Caldera: Coming from La Orotava, this site lies halfway up the hillside on the edge of the Aguamansa woods, near a trout farm. In the wood, near the 16.2 km marker, turn left. This well-equipped picnic site is now only a few minutes away, beside a small pond. The clearing is surrounded by fragrant woodland.

Chanajiga: Leave Puerto de la Cruz for Realejo Alto. Carry on to Cruz Santa and then turn left to Palo Blanco. After about 1.5 km, a track leads off to the hamlet of Las Llanadas, and the picnic site is signposted from here.

Las Arenas Negras: Make for Icod de los Vinos on the north coast and then carry on to La Montañeta. Higher up on the left-hand side stands a forest hut. Continue on foot to the picnic site, as the track is very bumpy. After a short climb through a pine wood, you'll find yourself in this magnificent recreational area.

Barranco de Ruiz: This small picnic site with a children's playground lies near the village of San Juan de la Rambla about halfway between Icod and Puerto de la Cruz, on the left-hand side near kilometre marker no. 48.

Carretera de Chío: Drive through the Cañadas towards the south and then turn left to Chío after the Llano de Ucanca plain. Pass through the huge area of lava and then after 10 km turn left to the

signposted picnic site and children's playground.

Los Roques: This large picnic site is situated beneath the bizarre Los Roques rock formation opposite the Parador Nacional. A short walk around the rocks starts here.

Las Raíces: Leave La Laguna along the Cumbre Dorsal and just beyond La Esperanza lies a 'historic' picnic site. General Franco once ate his packed lunch here! Turn left off the main road at kilometre marker 9. The site is about a kilometre further on.

Cumbres de Anaga: Drive from Las Mercedes towards the Anaga mountains. After a while you will come across a parallel road that runs to the left to Taganana and to San Andrés on the right. Carry straight on to the Mirador Bailadero, which offers a fine view down over Taganana. Follow the road to the hamlets of Lomo de las Bodegas, La Cumbrilla and Chamorga. The picnic site with its splendid views is just a little further on.

Las Lajas: Coming from Vilaflor, this picnic site is just beyond the Mirador Pino del Gordo. A further 10 km and you will be on the edge of Las Cañadas.

POST

The main post office in Puerto de la Cruz is situated in Calle del Pozo opposite the bus station, while the post office savings bank *(Caja Postal)* is in Calle Bethencourt. In Santa Cruz, the Caja Postal is located by the Plaza de España, in Los Cristianos in Calle Juan XXIII and in Playa de las Américas in Pueblo Canario *(11.00–14.00 hrs)*. Usual opening times: *Monday to Friday, 09.00–14.00, Saturday 09.00–13.00 hrs.* A 60-peseta stamp is required for letters and postcards to EU countries.

SAILING

For the committed amateur sailor, the Canary Islands have everything. The unbroken, warm, sunny weather means that the sailing season never ends, although the north coast is probably best avoided in winter. With the high mountains inland, the offshore winds can sometimes weaken to just a few infrequent gusts. On the other hand, the conditions along an inshore strip up to 10 km in width are not that pleasant. Between Gomera and Tenerife winds often blow strongly, with speeds of 35 knots not unusual. These weather conditions persist from November to February, when low pressure zones predominate over the archipelago, but the periods of strong winds only last from one to three days. The following harbours are easy to navigate and have good berths: Santa Cruz/Dársena Pesquera; Radazul marina; Candelaria fishing harbour; Puerto de Güímar leisure and fishing port; Poris de Abona fishing harbour; Las Galletas fishing harbour; Los Cristianos leisure harbour and the Puerto Colón marina in Playa de las Américas; Los Gigantes marina; Punta de Teno fishing harbour.

TAXIS

Taxis wait outside hotels and at designated ranks. Fares are charged according to the meter, but for many journeys a fixed fare applies which can be ascertained before departure. If you use the same taxi for a return journey you can get a reduced fare. Waiting time is accounted for separately. Taxis are available to tourists for excursions and it is often possible to negotiate a good price.

TELEPHONE

It is cheapest to phone from the light-blue public telephone booths (Cabina de Teléfono) and these accept most coins; however long-distance calls are best made using 100 pta coins. Phone cards are readily available and these are more convenient for international calls. To telephone abroad, dial 07 first and then wait for the high-pitched dialling tone. Then dial the relevant international code: United Kingdom 44, United States and Canada 1, Ireland 353.

TIME

In winter the Canary Islands observe Greenwich Mean Time; in summer they switch to British Summer Time.

TIPPING

In hotels and restaurants, service is usually included in the bill. However, a supplementary tip of 10% is the norm for hotel staff, waiting staff and taxi-drivers. This extra is discretionary and you are not obliged to pay it if you are not happy with the level of service or food you received.

VOLTAGE

Electrical appliances run on 220V in large hotels, 110V in the smaller pensions.

WEATHER IN SANTA CRUZ
Seasonal averages

Daytime temperatures in °C

Jan	Feb	Mar	Apr	May	June	July	Aug	Sep	Oct	Nov	Dec
21	21	22	23	24	26	28	29	28	26	23	22

Night-time temperatures in °C

Jan	Feb	Mar	Apr	May	June	July	Aug	Sep	Oct	Nov	Dec
14	14	15	16	17	19	21	21	21	19	17	16

Sunlight: hours per day

Jan	Feb	Mar	Apr	May	June	July	Aug	Sep	Oct	Nov	Dec
5	6	7	8	10	11	11	11	9	7	5	5

Rainfall: days per month

Jan	Feb	Mar	Apr	May	June	July	Aug	Sep	Oct	Nov	Dec
7	5	3	2	1	0	0	0	1	4	6	7

Sea temperatures in °C

Jan	Feb	Mar	Apr	May	June	July	Aug	Sep	Oct	Nov	Dec
19	18	18	18	19	20	21	22	23	23	21	20

Do's and Don'ts

Some of the traps and pitfalls that await the unwary traveller

Time-share touts

Do not be taken in by the time-share salesmen and women. If someone comes up to you, offers you a draw-ticket and then proclaims to whoops of delight that you have won the jackpot prize, be very wary. These are the sort of ploys that induce gullible holidaymakers to sign up for time-share accommodation deals that they can ill afford. Once an unsuspecting couple have been persuaded to visit a new time-share complex, highly-trained salespeople wear down their victims in such a way that they have little choice but to agree to the purchase of a fixed number of weeks in an apartment. For many people, the realization that they have been conned comes too late.

The carnation trick

If a pretty young woman approaches you on the street, embraces you and presents you with a carnation, beware. These attractive women insist on just one peseta for it. No other coin will do, but while you are rummaging around in your purse or wallet, they will help you in your search,

at the same time helping themselves (and with remarkable dexterity) to all the notes that are in there, too. And you probably won't know until it's too late.

Free bus rides

In the pedestrianized zones and other busy tourist spots, groups of young people spread out among the crowds and distribute handbills inviting you to visit one of the island's many attractions. If you are to believe what they say, you can go on one of the excursions at a very cheap price, sometimes for free, and you might even receive a present or win a prize. More often than not, these outings turn into shopping trips where sales personnel with persuasive techniques corner their victims and aggressively sell everyday items such as sheets and saucepans. In this situation it is easy to be forced into buying something you do not in fact want and, what is more, at an extortionate price that easily covers their publicity and transport costs. It is always better to book excursions through a travel agent or else hire a car.

INDEX

This index lists the main sights. The numbers in bold indicate a main entry.

95

What do you get for your money?

Given the frequent fluctuations in exchange rates, it's impossible to say exactly what your money is worth in pesetas. You won't be far wrong in your estimates if you reckon on 200 ptas to the pound or 125 ptas to the dollar. If you take Eurocheques or Travellers' Cheques, then you tend to get a better exchange rate than for cash. A number of banks and bureaux de change demand a high commission, so it's a good idea to shop around for the best rate.

The Spanish currency is the peseta. There are coins in denominations of 1 pta, 5 ptas, 10 ptas, 25 ptas, 50 ptas, 100 ptas, 200 ptas and 500 ptas and notes of 1000 ptas, 2000 ptas, 5000 ptas and 10000 ptas.

Prices vary greatly between the tourist regions and the rural villages. Here are a few examples: a coffee (café con leche) in Playa de las Américas will cost between 125 and 200 ptas, while in the interior it won't cost much more than 100 ptas; a bottle of beer in a simple bar might set you back 125-150 ptas, in a restaurant it will be 200 ptas; a bus trip from Puerto de la Cruz to Santa Cruz de Tenerife costs 750 ptas. Museum entrance prices can be anything up to 500 ptas and many have no entry fee. Simple set meals range from 900-1200 ptas, while a paella for two costs between 1600 and 2000 ptas.

The chart below will help you to make quick conversions, but for more exact and up-to-date rates you should check in the paper or high street bank before leaving.

£	Ptas	$
0.60	125	1.00
1.00	200	1.60
2.00	400	3.20
2.50	500	4.00
3.75	750	6.00
5.00	1000	8.00
10.00	2000	16.00
15.00	3000	24.00
20.00	4000	32.00
25.00	5000	40.00
50.00	10000	80.00
75.00	15000	120.00
100.00	20000	160.00
150.00	30000	240.00
200.00	40000	320.00
250.00	50000	400.00
500.00	100000	800.00